MY DAY! MY DREAM! MY DESTINY!

Date:

To:

From:

Message:

You Can Do More Than Survive, You Can Succeed!

EVERY DAY AN EASY A

Food Is for the Body
Education Is for the Mind
Poetry Is for the Soul

Sharon Esther Lampert

#1 Poetry Website for Student Projects
www.WorldFamousPoems.com
The Greatest Poems Ever Written
on Extraordinary World Events

The Restless Sunrise

A Streaming Golden Light
Enters In and Under the Windowsill

A Restless Sleeper
Is Awakened to New Beginnings

To Catch a Sunrise
The Dreamer Arises as the Light Bursts Forth

The Sunrise Lights Up the Sky
In Anticipation of a World

That Has Yet To Be Created.

Sharon Esther Lampert

Also By The Author

Student Empowerment Tools
for Academic Success

- EVERY DAY AN EASY A
- TOTAL RECALL: ACE EVERY TEST EVERY TIME
- Your Study Room Is Under New Management
- Smartgrades School Notebooks with 1000 Learning Tools
- WRITERS RUN THE WORLD: College English Bootcamp!
- LEARN ENGLISH

Parent Empowerment Tools
for Academic Success

- How to Parent for Academic Success
- Broken Wings Blocked Blessings

Teacher Empowerment Tools
for Academic Success

- The Silent Crisis Destroying America's Brightest Minds ("Book of the Month" Alma Public Library, Wisconsin)
- The Universal Gold Standard of Education
- How Does Learning Take Place

Psychological Empowerment Tools
for Academic Success

- Integration Therapy: 14 Steps to True and Everlasting Happiness
- How to Stop Paying for the Sins of Your Parents
- Lost, Bad, and Evil: The Root of All Evil Is Child Abuse

Children's Book
The Smartest Children's Book in The Whole World
Learn New Vocabulary with **Color-Coded** Words

SCHMALTZY: IN AMERICA EVEN A CAT CAN HAVE A DREAM
The Cat Who Helps Children Learn, Love, and Laugh
THE WORLD FAMOUS PIANO VIRTUOSO
BOOKWORM CHILDREN'S BOOK AWARD
schmaltzy.com

EVERY DAY AN EASY A

SMARTGRADES
BRAIN POWER REVOLUTION
www.smartgrades.com

SMARTGRADES SUCCESS STRATEGY/Elementary School Edition

EVERY DAY AN EASY A

©2024 @2012 by Sharon Rose Sugar. All Rights Reserved.
No part of this book may be used or reproduced in any manner whatsoever without written permission, except in the case of brief quotations embodied in critical articles and reviews.

Elementary School Edition
- Hardcover ISBN: 978-1-885872-93-7
- Paperback ISBN: 978-1-885872-94-4
- E-Book ISBN: 978-1-885872-12-8

Library of Congress Catalog Card Number: 2007902045
UPC: 672180

SMARTGRADES
BRAIN POWER REVOLUTION
Smartgrades.com
EverydayanEasyA.com
PhotonSuperhero.com
BooksnotBombs.com
Schmaltzy.com
SharonEstherLampert.com
WorldFamousPoems.com

SMARTGRADES books may be purchased for education, business, or sales promotional use.

To Order Books:
Ingram, Phone: 615-793-5000
Baker and Taylor, Phone: 800-775-1800

Book Interior and Cover Design By Sharon Esther Lampert
Illustrations: By Mark A. Hicks, illustrator. Used with permission.
For more information, please visit websites:
www.MARKIX.net and www.markix.net/4teachers.html

First Edition

Manufactured in the United States of America

8 Goalposts of Education

1. Education: Knowledge!
2. Enlightenment: AHA!
3. Empowerment: Yes I Can!
4. Excellence: Mastery!
5. Emancipation: All Can Do!
6. Egalitarianism: Equal Rights!
7. Equality: New World Order!
8. Economic Stability: World Peace!

Sharon Rose Sugar
The Paladin of Education for the 21st Century

To earn your diploma, every teacher will ask you to perform the same four academic tasks over and over again, day in and day out, week in and week out, and year in and year out.

1. Read a Chapter
2. Write a Paper
3. Solve a Problem
4. Take a Test

Sharon Rose Sugar
The Paladin of Education for the 21st Century

BOOK OF THE CENTURY
"The Silent Crisis Destroying America's Brightest Minds"
"Book of the Month" Alma Public Library, Wisconsin

READ, WRITE, SOLVE, TEST

EVERY DAY AN EASY A

SMARTGRADES
SUCCESS STRATEGY STUDY SKILLS

Our books include the **SMARTGRADES Learning Skills and Life Skills** that will empower you for academic success in school, personal success at home, and professional success in the workplace.

SMARTGRADES Time Management Skills:
- Homework Action Planner
- To Do List Tool
- Setting Priorities Tool
- Divide and Conquer Tool
- Estimate and Actual Time Log Tool
- Speedbumps: Detours, Delays, and Distractions Tool

SMARTGRADES In-Class Skills:
- Prereading Tool
- Active Listening Tool
- Note Taking Tool
- Abbreviation Tool
- Questioning Tool
- Test Preview Question Tool

SMARTGRADES At-Home Skills:
- Organization Tool
- School Notebooks with **SMARTGRADES SUCCESS STRATEGY**
- Study Room Tool
- Study Strategy Tool
- Subject Strategy Tool
- Power Study Snack Tool

SMARTGRADES Reading Skills:
- Speed Reading Tool
- Reading Comprehension Tool

SMARTGRADES Test Preparation Tools:
- Processing Tools for Instant & Total Recall

SMARTGRADES Writing Skills:
- Outlining Tool
- Annotating Tool
- Summarizing Tool
- Paraphrasing Tool
- English Essay Tool
- Research Paper Tool
- Citation Tool
- Proofreading to Perfection Tool

SMARTGRADES Thinking Skills:
- Critical Thinking Tool
- Creative Thinking Tool **WORLD PREMIERE!**
- Scientific Thinking Tool
- Mathematical Thinking Tool

SMARTGRADES On-Test Skills:
- Multiple Choice Tool
- Essay Exam Tool
- True False Tool
- Matching Tool
- Fill In the Blank Tool
- Identity Exam Tool
- Verbal Analogy Tool
- Oral Exam Tool
- Open Book Tool
- Take Home Tool
- Standardized Exam Tool

SMARTGRADES Career Skills:
- Career and Personality Tool
- Summer Internship & Life Experience Tool
- Networking Tool
- Entrepreneur Tool
- Job Tool
- Career Tool

© 2000. All Rights Reserved. **SMARTGRADES INC.**

EVERY DAY AN EASY A

Sugar's 7 Grade A Facts of Academic Success

Fact 1. Your Brain Is a Powerful Biological Machine
Put your hands on your head and feel your brain. Your brain is the most powerful biological machine in the world. This book is your instruction manual and will show you how to maximize your brain power. Facts are food for the brain. You will spend most of your day eating facts and building your brain muscles. First, you will receive facts from your teacher. Second, you will process the facts using the new learning technology, SMART-GRADES Success Strategy, . Third, you will return the facts to the teacher in a essay, research paper, or on a test.

Fact 2. Eat Right for the Energy to Learn (Chapter 3)
Before you can feed your brain the facts, you have to feed your body for the energy to learn. Healthy meals consist of carbohydrates, protein, fresh fruits and vegetables containing vitamins and minerals. To maximize your energy to learn, you will need sufficient sleep, good eating habits, and regular exercise. Junk food won't cut it. Avoid eating foods loaded with addictive sugar and salt and processed with chemicals that are devoid of natural vitamins and minerals.

Fact 3. The First Week of School (Chapter 1)
It only takes the first week of school for students to fall behind and start playing catch-up. You have to learn how to manage your time, and make every hour count.

Fact 4. School Is All About the Facts, Not About You
Your job is to **RETRIEVE** the facts from the class notes, handouts, and textbook, and then **RETURN** the facts to the teacher in an essay, research paper, and on a test.

SMARTGRADES BRAIN POWER REVOLUTION

Fact 5. The 80/20 Rule (Chapter 7)
If you can send back 80% of the facts for a B grade, then you can send back the remaining 20% of the facts for an A grade. If you process the facts for long-term retention using the new learning technology, SMARTGRADES SUCCESS STRATEGY, then you will have Instant & Total Recall of all of the facts.

Fact 6. What Are the Critical Hours of the School Day?
- Class Time: 1 Hour (fixed) RETRIEVE FACTS
- Study Period: 2-6 Hours (variable) "EAT" FACTS
- Test Time:1 Hour (fixed) RETURN FACTS

Fact 7. Every Day of the Week Is Test Preparation Day
Priority #1 Did you sleep well, eat right, and exercise for the energy to learn? (Chapter 3)

Priority #2 Do you have a SMARTGRADES Planner to manage your life? (Chapter 1 & 2)

Priority #3 Do you have SMARTGRADES School Notebooks that contain processing tools to write papers to perfection and ace every test every time? (Chapter 4)

Priority #4 Right after class, did you write Test-Review Notes and process the facts using your SMARTGRADES Success Strategy, for Instant & Total Recall to ace every test? (Chapter 7)

10 STEP SMARTGRADES SUCCESS STRATEGY STUDY SKILLS:

Step 1. Estimation	Step 6. Association
Step 2. Divide and Conquer	Step 7. Test Review Notes
Step 3. Active Reading	Step 8. Conversion
Step 4. Extraction	Step 9. Visualization
Step 5. Condensation	Step 10. Self-Test

SUPERHIGHWAY OF ACADEMIC SUCCESS

1. School Is All About the Facts

2. The Facts Are Always on the Move

In Class
Facts Move from a Blackboard into a Notebook

At Home
Facts Move into a Test Review Note,
Homework Assignment, Essay, and Research Paper

On Test
Facts Move Through Your Brain for Instant
and Total Recall and onto a Test

Education Is Measured by 3 Criteria:
In-Depth Comprehension
Long Term Retention
Mastery of the Material

Sharon Rose Sugar
The Paladin of Education for the 21st Century

THIS BOOK SAVES LIVES
"The Silent Crisis Destroying America's Brightest Minds"
"Book of the Month" Alma Public Library, Wisconsin

Attention All Earthlings!

Put Your Hands on Your Head.
Your Brain Is the Most Powerful
Biological Machine in the World.
Your Brain Is Your Most Valuable Asset.
This Book Is the Instruction Manual for Your Brain.

Facts Are Food for Your Brain.
School Is a Restaurant and Facts Are on the Menu.
Eat the Facts and Build Your Brain Muscle.
Knowledge Is Power, Purpose, Passion, and Prosperity.
Good Grades Deserve Great Rewards.
In 24 Hours, Earn A Grade, Earn Free Gift!

Make the Grade and Achieve Your Dream!
Every Student Is a Success Story!
Every Student Is Somebody Special!
MY DAY! MY DREAM! MY DESTINY!
LIVE YOUR DREAMS!

If You Need My Help, I Am at Your Service,

www.PhotonSuperhero.com

**MY DAY!
MY DREAM!
MY DESTINY!**

Contents

Chapter 1
Take Control of Your Time
"Better Three Hours Too Soon, Than One Minute Too Late."
~ William Shakespeare
25

Chapter 2
Multiple Schedules
Make Big Plans and Take Small Steps
"Don't Count Every Hour in the Day,
Make Every Hour in the Day Count."
~ Unknown
47

Chapter 3
Eat Right for the Energy to Learn, Laugh, and Love
"Energy Is Eternal Delight."
~ William Blake
55

Chapter 4
Take Control of the Facts
Organize the Mountain of Academic Materials
"For Every Minute Spent Organizing, an Hour is Earned."
~ Unknown
65

Chapter 5
Manage Your Worry, Anxiety, Stress,
and Bouts of Depression
"Pressure Turns Coal into Diamonds."
~ Unknown
77

Chapter 6
Get the Most Out of Class
"First Learn to Listen and Then Listen to Learn."
~ Unknown
91

Chapter 7
SMARTGRADES PROCESSING TOOLS
ACE EVERY TEST EVERY TIME
Write Test Review Notes, Instant & Total Recall, Ace Test
"A Room Without Books Is Like a Body Without a Soul."
~ Marcus Tullius Cicero
107

Chapter 8
Read, Write, and Proofread
"I Hate Writing. I Love Having Written."
~ Dorothy Parker
131 (Writing) 165 (Proofreading)

Chapter 9
Read, Memorize, and Test
"Failing to Prepare Is Preparing to Fail"
~ Unknown
173

Chapter 10
Critical Brain Power Tools
"There Is Only One Truth. No One Has the Truth."
~ Sharon Esther Lampert
195

Chapter 11
WORLD PREMIERE!
Creative Brain Power Tools: 10 Esoteric Laws of Creativity
"**ART** IS OF THE HE**ART**"
~ Sharon Esther Lampert
201

Chapter 12
Scientific Brain Power Tools
"Theory Guides. Experiment Decides."
~ Unknown
207

Chapter 13
Mathematical Brain Power Tools
"If You Think Dogs Can't Count, Try Putting Three Dog Biscuits in Your Pocket and Then Giving Fido Only Two of Them."
~Phil Pastoret
211

Chapter 14
What Do You Want to Be When You Grow Up?
219

A Journey of a Thousand Miles Begins with a Single Step

Lao-Tzu
The Way of Lao-Tzu
Chinese Philosopher (604 BC-531 BC)

Chapter 1
Take Control of Your Time

Time Works For and Against Us
Depending Upon How We Use It

Israeli Prime Minister David Ben Gurion

Chapter 1
Take Control of Your Time

Tools of the Trade
SMARTGRADES Homework Action Planner

Steps to Success

Step 1. Write the words **Daily Action Plan** at top of page.

Step 2. Write a **To Do List** of big goal and small steps.

Step 3. **Set Your Priorities:** Urgent, Important, Low, and Optional.

Step 4. **Divide and Conquer:** Break down big tasks into smaller more manageable tasks.

Step 5. Use Time Logs: **Estimated Time** and **Actual Time.**

Step 6. Life is a bumpy road lined with speedbumps. Make time for delays, detours, and distractions.

Step 7. Use checkboxes to keep track of completed tasks.

Step 8. Don't leave home without your **To Do List**.

Step 9. At the end of each day, review your game plan and refine it. Pay attention to your strengths and weaknesses.

Step 10. Celebrate a job well done with a daily reward.

EVERY DAY AN EASY A

Plan Your Work and Work Your Plan

Don't Wish For It, Work For It

Success Comes in Cans, Not Cants

Well Done Is Better Than Well Said

The Only Something You Get for Nothing Is Failure

When You Lose, Don't Lose the Lesson

Do What You Love, Love What You Do

Step 1: Write a Daily Action Plan

Eat Right for the Energy to Learn:
Breakfast: Lunch: Dinner:

Daily Budget: $
Expense 1. $ Expense 2. $ Expense 3. $
Total Daily Expenses: $

Classes:
Subject: Time: Room:
Subject: Time: Room:

Study Period 1: (45 minutes each with 15 minute breaks)
Time: Study Area:
❏ Eat study snacks to stay energized, e.g., bananas, oranges
❏ Read class notes, handouts, and textbook
❏ Write Test Review Notes: Use **SMARTGRADES** Processing Tools

---

Daily Exercise Routine: Stretch, Aerobics, Weights, Stretch

Study Period 2: (45 minutes each with 15 minute breaks)
❏ Seek approval from teacher for outline of paper
❏ Preread tomorrow's chapter to prepare for class

Read a Daily Funny for Stress-Relief: "HA, HA, HA"

Part-Time Job:

Family Chores:

Social Life:

Regular Bedtime: 10 p.m.   Actual Bedtime:

Daily Reward for a Job Well Done:

Best Part of Day:

Worst Part of Day: Speedbumps: Delays, Detours, Distractions?

Step 2: Write a "To Do List"

Dreams Are Goals with Deadlines

Your **To Do List** consists of two kinds of lists, namely, the big picture or big idea, and the myriad of details.

TO DO LIST

BIG PICTURE
MANY DETAILS

For example, if you are going to the gym, your **To Do List** will probably look a lot like this one.

To Do List

Big Picture: Go to Gym: 1-2 p.m.

Many Details
- ☐ 1. Membership I.D.
- ☐ 2. Water bottle to stay hydrated
- ☐ 3. Weight lifting belt and gloves
- ☐ 4. music, headphones, check battery
- ☐ 5. Bring towel, shampoo, and comb
- ☐ 6. Vaseline and baby powder to reduce feet friction
- ☐ 7. Knee support brace

Step 3: Set Priorities
Urgent, Important, Low, and Optional

Write a **To Do List** that includes the big picture and the myriad of details, and assign one of the priorities below to each task.

Urgent
Cannot be postponed, immediate or emergency

Important
Needs attention today, but is not an emergency

Low
Can be put off until later in the week

Optional
Can be crossed off the list or postponed indefinately

For example, here are a list of tasks that need to be completed after school:

To Do List
- 1. Walk dog
- 2. Write English essay due tomorrow
- 3. Pick up groceries for dinner
- 4. Mail letter at post office
- 5. Buy fresh flowers for dinner table

Set Priorities

Prioritize the tasks by writing down one of the words from the list on the previous page.

To Do List
- 1. Walk dog: **URGENT**
- 2. Write English essay due tomorrow: **URGENT**
- 3. Pick up groceries for dinner: **IMPORTANT**
- 4. Mail a letter at post office: **LOW**
- 5. Buy fresh flowers for dinner table: **OPTIONAL**

URGENT: The dog has to be walked and the English essay has to be written today. Let's see how many tasks we can complete by spending a few minutes analyzing the list.

Choice 1. What if we walk the dog in the direction of the post office and mail the letter, and then on the way back from the post office, we walk by the florist and pick up some flowers for the dinner table.

To Do List

☐ 1. Walk dog: **URGENT**
☐ 2. Mail letter at post office: **LOW**
☐ 3. Buy fresh flowers for dinner table: **OPTIONAL**
☐ 4. Write English essay due tomorrow: **IMPORTANT**

Choice 2. Or we can walk the dog and mail the letter tomorrow and cross the flowers off the list for today. We have to bring the dog home before we can go to the store and pick up groceries or call a take-out restaurant for a delivery.

To Do List

☐ 1. Walk dog: **URGENT**
☐ 2. Pick up groceries for dinner: **IMPORTANT**
☐ 3. Write English essay due tomorrow: **URGENT**

DAILY ACTION PLAN

Make a detailed **To Do List** and set your priorities to meet your **URGENT** and **IMPORTANT** deadlines. If you can squeeze in the **LOW** and **OPTIONAL** tasks, then do so. If not, postpone them or cross them off the list.

Step 4: Divide and Conquer

Break Down Big Tasks into Smaller More Manageable Tasks

Most tasks have many steps. Each step takes a different amount of time to do. Some tasks appear overwhelming. When that happens, procrastination sets in. We can't seem to get started because the task requires too many steps, and there are many speed bumps along the way.

To Do List

Step 1. Write down the GOAL

Step 2. Write down STEPS required to achieve GOAL

Step 3. Set your priorities: **URGENT, IMPORTANT, LOW**

Step 4. Keep breaking down big tasks into smaller tasks

For example, I want to go to the gym to exercise. There are many steps involved. Here is my **To Do List** of the tasks that need to be accomplished before I can exercise.

To Do List: Join a Gym

- ☐ Priority 1. Purchase a gym membership
- ☐ Priority 2. Purchase a workout outfit and sneakers
- ☐ Priority 3. Purchase weight-lifting gloves
- ☐ Priority 4. Download music from iTunes

- ☐ Priority 5. Purchase book containing workout routines
- ☐ Priority 6. Purchase water bottle to stay hydrated
- ☐ Priority 7. Purchase gym bag to hold water bottle, exercise book, keys, I.D., and towel
- ☐ Priority 8. Go to gym to exercise

You will have to make another **To Do List** of exercises to get you into great shape, as follows:

To Do List: My Workout Routine
- ☐ Step 1. Stretch for 10 minutes to warm-up
- ☐ Step 2. Ride stationary bike for 15 minutes
- ☐ Step 3. Run on treadmill for 15 minutes
- ☐ Step 4. Do 25 sit-ups
- ☐ Step 5. Use weight machines for 30 minutes
- ☐ Step 6. Stretch for 10 minutes to cool down

You may decide that going to the gym is too complicated a task, and that you would rather take a half hour walk or ride your bicycle to get some aerobic activity and keep your heart in great shape.

To Do List: Ride Bike Around Park
- ☐ Step 1. Check air in tires
- ☐ Step 2. Check brakes
- ☐ Step 3. Stay hydrated, bring water bottle and snack
- ☐ Step 4. Ride bike along trail in park for 1 mile

Divide and Conquer: Every task needs to be broken down into smaller tasks, to make them more manageable and easier to complete. Let's take a closer look at each of the goals featured below.

Main Goal 1. Purchase Gym Membership

Divide and Conquer:

- ☐ 1. Call and make an appointment to speak to an agent
- ☐ 2. Meet with agent and take a tour of gym
- ☐ 3. Sign contract and pay with credit card/cash
- ☐ 4. Comb hair and prepare for photograph
- ☐ 5. Pose for photograph for a membership I.D.

Main Goal 2. Purchase workout outfit

Divide and Conquer:

- ☐ 1. Go to store and look for workout outfit
- ☐ 2. Try on outfit to see how it fits
- ☐ 3. Look for another outfit that fits better
- ☐ 4. Try on different outfits to find the best fit
- ☐ 5. Stand on a long checkout line to purchase outfit
- ☐ 6. Find new shelf space for outfit in cluttered closet

Main Goal 3. Purchase digital music to stay motivated

Divide and Conquer:

- ☐ 1. Go online and research workout music
- ☐ 2. Choose right artist, tempo, and lyrics
- ☐ 3. Download songs to cellphone

For Example: Write a School Paper
Your teacher will either assign an essay or a research paper, and each academic task needs to be broken down into smaller more manageable tasks, as follows:

Big Task: Write an English essay for class on abortion

Divide and Conquer:
- ☐ Step 1. Use encyclopedia for general overview of topic.

- ☐ Step 2. Read bibliographic citations to find experts in field and primary and secondary source materials.

- ☐ Step 3. Read primary sources for pro and con arguments.

- ☐ Step 4. Choose a position and write a thesis statement.

- ☐ Step 5. Write outline of main ideas and supporting examples.

- ☐ Step 6. Use outline to write rough draft of paper.

Divide and Conquer: Always break down big tasks that appear to be overwhelming into smaller tasks that are easier to navigate. This is the antidote for bouts of procrastination that can paralyze and cripple productivity, and derail academic success.

EVERY DAY AN EASY A

Step 5. Use Time Logs

Write down "Estimated" and "Actual" Time

To take control of your time, you have to write down two different measurements:

Estimated Time (Fantasy)   Actual Time (Reality)

Estimated Time (Fantasy, Wishful Thinking)
The first amount of time is the estimated time. This is the time you would like the task to take. This time is usually a miscalculation because of the speedbumps.

Actual Time (Time Plus Life's Inevitable Setbacks)
The second amount of time is the actual time. Most tasks will take longer to accomplish because life is a bumpy road of setbacks (this is normal). In "REAL LIFE" there are many speed bumps called delays, detours, and distractions that will slow you down and get in your way.

For example: Write a Research Paper
Step 1.	Choose a topic and title	1/2 Hour
Step 2.	Do research	5 Hours
Step 3.	Write outline	1 Hour
Step 4.	Write rough and final draft	10 Hours
Step 5.	Proofread paper to perfection	2 Hours

Time Log
Estimated Time: 18 1/2 Hours
Actual Time: 20 1/2 Hours
Error: 2 hours (trip to store, no ink, out of paper)

Delay: My printer ran out of ink and I had to stop at the store to pick up a new cartridge.

Detour: The store was closed and I had to wait until the next day to pick up the ink to print out my paper.

Distraction: On the way to the store, I passed my favorite pizza shop and decided to grab a quick slice.

On one hand, your class time and test time are easy to manage because they have fixed times:

Go to class: 1 hour per class (fixed)   Actual Time
Take a test: 1 hour per test (fixed)   Actual Time

On the other hand, your study schedule will be difficult to manage because different assignments take different amounts of time to complete. Your assignments have variable times, as folllows:

Academic Assignments:
1. End of Chapter Questions   2-3 Hours (variable)
2. English Essay   5-10 Hours (variable)
3. Research Report   10-25 Hours (variable)
4. Test Preparation   5-25 Hours (variable)

EVERY DAY AN EASY A

Let's apply our **SMARTGRADES** Time Management Tools to our English essay assignment, as follows:

First: We create a **To Do List** (big picture and details).
Second: We set priorities: urgent, important, and low.
Third: We break down the big task into smaller tasks.
Fourth: We add estimated and actual time logs.
Fifth: We record speedbumps: delays, detours, and distractions.
Sixth: We use checkboxes for completed tasks.
Seventh: We celebrate a job well done with a reward.

Big Academic Task
Write a 5 Page English Essay

Steps to Success

☐ Step 1. Use encyclopedia for general overview of topic
Time Log
Estimated Time: 1 Hour
Actual Time:
Speedbumps: Any Delays, Detours, and Distractions?

☐ Step 2. Read bibliographic citations for experts in field and primary and secondary source materials
Time Log
Estimated Time: 45 Minutes
Actual Time:
Speedbumps: Any Delays, Detours, and Distractions?

☐ Step 3. Read primary sources for pro and con arguments
Time Log
Estimated Time: 5 Hours
Actual Time:
Speedbumps: Any Delays, Detours, and Distractions?

☐ Step 4. Write outline of main ideas and supporting details
Time Log
Estimated Time: 3 Hours
Actual Time:
Speedbumps: Any Delays, Detours, and Distractions?
_____

☐ Step 5. Meet with teacher for approval of outline
Time Log
Estimated Time: 1/2 Hour
Actual Time:
Speedbumps: Any Delays, Detours, and Distractions?
_____

☐ Step 6. Use outline to write rough draft of paper
Time Log
Estimated Time: 10 Hours
Actual Time:
Speedbumps: Any Delays, Detours, and Distractions?
_____

☐ Step 7. Meet with teacher for approval of rough draft
Time Log
Estimated Time: 1 Hour
Actual Time:
Speedbumps: Any Delays, Detours, and Distractions?
_____

☐ Step 8. Write final draft and proofread to perfection
Time Log
Estimated Time: 10 Hours
Actual Time:
Speedbumps: Any Delays, Detours, and Distractions?
_____☐

Step 9. Hand in paper and earn an A grade. Celebrate.

Step 6. Setbacks
Life Is a Bumpy Road of
Delays, Detours, and Distractions

Setbacks are inevitable. There are many different types of setbacks. Life is a bumpy road of delays, detours, and distractions that have to be anticipated and calculated.

Delays: You keep miscalculating the "Real Time" it takes to complete a goal.

Detours: You are supposed to go to the tutoring center to ask for help, but your friend calls and invites you to a game.

Distractions: You are looking for one article on the internet but find yourself distracted by tabloid gossip.

At the end of each day, look at your **Daily Action Plan** and see what is working and what is not working.

Q. What types of **delays** are taking your time?
A. The subway is faster than the bus or taxi due to traffic
Q. What types of **detours** are taking your time?
A. Spending too much time socializing with friends
Q. What types of **distractions** are taking your time?
A. I am watching too many reality TV shows on weeknights

Less is More Is One Key to Success

Doing less is a good idea. Don't try to squeeze too many activities into one day. Spread your activities over a longer period of time. Instead of thinking daily, think weekly, monthly, or yearly for some of the things you want to accomplish. Take baby steps each and every day toward a goal that you will reach by the end of the year.

- Daily Test Review Notes: **SMARTGRADES SUCCESS STRATEGY**
- Exercise three times a week
- Have dinner with family once a week
- Go to a sporting event once a month
- Visit museum exhibit every six months

Simplicity is One Key to Success

Keep each day as simple as possible. Streamline your life for simplicity. Simplicity is making a **Daily Action Plan** that contains only life's necessities.

- ☐ 1. Eat Right for Energy to Learn (whole grains)
- ☐ 2. Sleep Well for Energy to Learn (8 Hours)
- ☐ 3. Exercise for Energy to Learn (1/2 Hr. walk)
- ☐ 4. Go to Class and then Write a Test Review Note
- ☐ 5. Ace Tests with Your **SMARTGRADES SUCCESS STRATEGY**
- ☐ 6. Call Home: **"Mom, I Earned an A Grade Today"**
- ☐ 7. Celebrate Success with a Reward for a Job Well Done

EVERY DAY AN EASY A

Let's Recap: How to Take Control of Your Time

1. **Write a To Do List of the Big Picture and Add Details**

    Big Picture: Write an English Essay

    1. Choose a Researchable Topic
    2. Do Research
    3. Write Outline
    4. Write a Rough and Final Draft
    5. Proofread to Perfection

---

2. **Set Your Priorities:**
    1. Urgent (Do Now)
    2. Important (Do Today)
    3. Low (Leave for Another Day)
    4. Optional (Cross off List)

---

3. **Divide and Conquer: Breakdown Big Task -> Smaller Tasks**
    1. **Choose Topic**
        a. Choose a topic that is researchable
    2. **Research Topic**
        a. Use encyclopedia for a general overview of topic
        b. Read for experts in the field
        c. Read for pro and con arguments
        d. Read bibliographic citations for primary source materials
    3. **Write an Outline**
        a. List the main ideas and supporting pro and con arguments

4. Write Down Time Logs: Estimated and Actual Time

☐ Step 1. Read encyclopedia for experts in field
Estimated Time: 1 Hour
Actual Time:
Error Time:
Speedbumps: Any Delays, Detours, and Distractions?

☐ Step 2. Read the primary source material
Estimated Time: 5 Hours
Actual Time:
Error Time:
Speedbumps: Any Delays, Detours, and Distractions?

☐ Step 3. Make a list of pro and con arguments
Estimated Time: 3 Hours
Actual Time:
Error Time:
Speedbumps: Any Delays, Detours, and Distractions?

5. Use Checkboxes to Keep Track of Completed Tasks

☐ 1. ☐ 2.

6. Review Your Game Plan and Refine it. Pay Attention to Your Strengths and Weaknesses.

Strength: Right after class, I wrote Test Review Notes

Weakness: Wasted 2 hours on internet tabloid gossip

Step 7: Celebrate a Job Well Done with a Daily Reward

Today's Reward: Movie night

Mile by Mile, Life's a Trial.
Yard by Yard, It's Not So Hard.
Inch by Inch, It's a Cinch

Chapter 2
Multiple Schedules
Make Big Plans and Take Small Steps

The Key is Not to Prioritize What's on Your Schedule, But to Schedule Your Priorities

Stephen Covey

Chapter 2

Multiple Schedules
Make Big Plans and Take Small Steps

Your life will revolve around ten different types of schedules and you will need to write them down, analyze them, and reconfigure them, so that there is a seamless flow between them, instead of conflict, confusion, and chaos.

Schedule 1. Eat Right for Energy to Learn (variable)

Schedule 2. Class Schedule (fixed)

Schedule 3. Study Schedule (variable)

Schedule 4. Test Schedule (fixed)

Schedule 5. Family Chores Schedule (variable)

Schedule 6. Extra-Curricular School Activities (variable)

Schedule 7. Playdate Schedule (variable)

Schedule 8. Free Time (variable and negligible)

My Multiple Schedules Worksheet

Schedule 1. Eat Right for the Energy to Learn (variable)
M: Whole grains, protein, fresh fruits, and vegetables
T:
W:
T:
F:
S:
S:

Schedule 2. Class Schedule (fixed)

M:

T:

W:

T:

F:

Schedule 3. Study Periods (variable)
M: Right after school, write your Test Review Notes
T:
W:
T:
F:
S:
S:

Schedule 4. Test Schedule (fixed)
M:
T:
W:
T:
F:
S:
S:

Schedule 5. Family Responsibilities (variable)
M:
T:
W:
T:
F:
S:
S:

Schedule 6. Extra-Curricular Activities (fixed)
M:
T:
W:
T:
F:
S:
S:

Schedule 7. Playdates (variable)
M:　School night
T:　　School night
W:　School night
T:　School night
F:
S:
S:

Schedule 8. Free Time (variable and negligible)
M:
T:
W:
T:
F:
S:
S:

Take Control of Your Social Life Schedule

Keeping in touch with friends takes time. Pick a time to chat with your friends. Don't answer the phone and interrupt your study period every time a friend calls to talk with you, unless that friend is your study buddy. Pick a time after your school work is completed to make your social calls and stay connected to your loved ones.

Examples:

1. Suzy called about making a plan to see a movie

Action Plan: Call her back at 9:30 P.M.

Time Log

Estimated Time: 10 Minutes

Actual Time: 1 1/2 Hours

Error: 1 Hour and 20 Minutes

Delays, Detours, and Distractions: School Gossip

Action Plan: Friday, 8 P.M. for movie, meet at cafe

2. Peter called to study for test, study buddy

Action Plan: Call him back at 7:45 P.M.

Time Log

Estimated Time:

Actual Time:

Error:

Delays, Detours, and Distractions:

Action Plan: Meet in school library, Tuesday, 2 P.M.

My Social Life Schedule (Variable)

Making new friends and keeping in touch with old friends takes time. Your friends will change over time and place.

Q: How often do you introduce yourself to a new person?
a. Daily   b. Weekly   c. Monthly   d. Yearly

Here's how to introduce yourself to a new person:
1. Smile and make eye contact.
2. Say "Hello."
3. Ask a simple question? "What time do you have?"
4. Offer a compliment: "I love your blue sweater."
5. Introduce yourself: "My name is . . ."
6. What's your name?
7. Find common ground:
a. New study buddy
b. New playdate
c. New teammate for sports
d. New movie friend, loves comedy

Great relationships are based on connection, chemistry, compatibility, caring, communication, companionship, and common ground. When you meet someone, take notes:
Q1. What kind of connection do we have?
Q2. Do we have chemistry?
Q3. Are we compatible?
Q4. Is there genuine affection between us?
Q5. Do we have common interests?
Q6. Do we have honest communication?

The Energy of the Mind
Is the Essence of Life

Aristotle
Ancient Greek Philosopher, Scientist, and Physician
384 BC-322 BC

Chapter 3
Eat Right for the Energy to Learn, Laugh, and Love

EVERY DAY AN EASY A

Q: Are You Hungry for the Energy to Learn?
Whole Grain High Fiber Breakfast
Power Lunch: (Big Plate)
Lite Dinner: (Small Plate)
Power Study Snacks

Chapter 3
Eat for Energy to Learn, Laugh, and Love

Q1. What Did You Eat this Morning?

You can't learn on an empty stomach. It takes energy to learn. Energy comes from good nutrition and sufficient sleep. First you feed your body with food, and then you feed your mind with facts.

Your electrical appliances will not work without a boost of electricity, and your brain will not work without a boost of whole grain fiber, protein, fresh fruits and vegetables loaded with natural (not synthetic) vitamins and minerals.

Think of yourself as a car with a gas tank that has to be filled up to be able to take you places. First, you fill your tank and then you drive. First, you eat a nutritious meal and then you go to school to learn. If you don't eat properly, your brain will not have the "FULL GAS TANK" to be able to read, think, question, research, write, memorize, and test.

Q2. Did You Put Some Love Into It?

Learning requires love. You have to put love into everything that you do. Your heart and your mind have to be working together as a team. According to the poet, philosopher, and educator, Sharon Esther Lampert, "You don't find love, you create love." Love has to be created. Like a warm and cozy fire on a cold winter's night, you have to create love for it to exist in the world.

Q3. Did You Laugh Today?

Learning requires a sense of humor. The learning curve is steep. It takes time to learn. Learning requires trial'n'error. Learning requires patience and practice until mastery is achieved. Sometimes you will have to get it all wrong, before you can get it all right. It is best to not take yourself so seriously, and to learn to laugh at yourself from time to time as you will often stumble blindly in the dark trying to figure out what your strengths and weaknesses are, where you belong in the world, and how you can make a difference and, ultimately, a contribution of meaningful significance.

Try not to let a day go by without a laugh that will bring a smile to your face. Late night TV talk shows use the daily newspaper as a spring board for spinning human trials and tribulations into comedy. The day may start out bleakly, but it always ends with a laugh. But don't stay up late to watch these TV shows, rather watch the reruns on the internet the next day, and go to bed at a decent hour. Almost every TV show is recorded on the internet, so you can watch them at your convenience, when you need a study break and a good laugh.

The Best Study Break Is the Website T.E.D.

T.E.D. is a website showcasing interesting people in the world, who make a difference. These people are hardly ever featured on TV. These people will inspire you, as you embark on your own academic journey in search of a purpose in life that is imbued with passion and prosperity.

Change Your Knowledge Base

Quite often, you will have to change your "Knowledge Base." To move forward in the world, you will have to leave the past behind, and get on a new road that will take you to a new place that is entirely different from where you came from and what you were taught.

Old Knowledge Base: "I can eat anything I want, as long as I eat in moderation."

New Knowledge Base: "I can't eat anything I want because the processed food is loaded with salt, sugar, corn syrup, and a whole host of chemicals and preservatives that I can't pronounce, spell, or remember.

Here are a few of the consequences of eating processed food:

- My body will not have sufficient vitamins and minerals

- I will always feel tired and want to eat more junk

- My body will overeat processed food trying to get energy from the food

- I will become overweight and undernourished

New Knowledge Base: Avoid Processed Food

I will not eat anything wrapped in plastic that can live for more than ten years in my knapsack, including those packaged protein bars (loaded with sugar).

How to Eat Right for the Energy to Learn

You are a biological machine that needs fiber fuel to be able to think, read, research, write, memorize, and test. Before you leave for school, you need to have a system in place to manage your energy needs.

The Fiber Facts
Whole Grain Foods = Long-Term Energy and No Cravings

My 30-Second Breakfast
- Grab a bran muffin (try a different flavor each day)
- Grab two hard-boiled eggs (protein)
- Grab fruit: banana, apple, and orange (vitamins)
- Grab a container of orange juice (hydration)

My One-Minute Breakfast
- A slice of whole grain toast, cheese, tomato (fiber)
- Grab two hard-boiled eggs (protein)
- Grab fruit: banana, apple, and orange (vitamins)
- Grab a container of orange juice (hydration)

My Five-Minute Breakfast (Breakfast of Champions)
- A bowl of delicious and creamy oatmeal, add walnuts, sliced banana, cinnamon, and maple syrup. Drink a glass of orange juice.

My Power Lunch (Big Plate)

Fill big plate with 1/4 fist-sized protein and 3/4 vegetables

Monday: Fish with spinach, carrots, grilled red peppers
Tuesday: Meat with broccoli, carrots, corn
Wednesday: Fish with spinach, carrots, cauliflower
Thursday: Meat with green beans, carrots, corn
Friday: Fish with spinach, carrots, grilled red pepper

My Lite Dinner (Small Plate)

Fill small plate with 1/4 fist-sized protein and 3/4 vegetables

1. Eat off of a small plate to reduce your portion size
2. Eat dinner before 7 p.m.
3. Fill up on salad, vegetable soup, steamed vegetables
4. Avoid fried, fatty, and greasy food
5. Avoid heavy foods that put you to sleep after a meal
6. Avoid foods with sugar that keep you up late at night
7. No caffeinated drinks after 5 p.m. (poor sleep)

My Power Study Snacks for the Energy to Learn

1. Golden delicious apples with peanut butter or cheese
2. Fresh berries with yogurt and nuts, add honey
3. Carrot and celery sticks with humus
4. Bran muffins (cranberry, banana, carrot, apple)

Make Your Own Food Plan for the Energy to Learn

My 30-Second Breakfast

Whole Grain Fiber (long lasting fuel, no cravings):

_____

Protein: _____

Vegetables: _____

Fruits: _____

Hydration (sugar free): _____

My One-Minute Breakfast

Whole Grain Fiber (long lasting fuel, no cravings):

_____

Protein: _____

Vegetables: _____

Fruits: _____

Hydration (sugar free): _____

My Five-Minute Breakfast

Whole Grain Fiber (long lasting fuel, no cravings):

_____

Protein: _____

Vegetables: _____

Fruits: _____

Hydration (sugar free): _____

My Power Lunch (Big Plate)

Protein: Fish/Meat/Beans _____

Vegetables: _____

Fruits: _____

Hydration (sugar free): _____

Low Fat Dessert: _____

My Lite Dinner (Small Plate for Small Portions)

Protein: Fish/Meat/Bean _____

Vegetables: _____

Fruits: _____

Hydration (sugar free): _____

Low Fat Dessert: _____

No Caffeine After 5 P.M. (poor sleep, tired next day)

My Power Study Snacks for the Energy to Learn

Monday: _____

Tuesday: _____

Wednesday: _____

Thursday: _____

Friday: _____

Saturday: _____

Sunday: _____

A Place for Everything, Everything in its Place

Benjamin Franklin

Chapter 4
Organize the Mountain of Academic Materials

Don't Agonize, Organize!
Florynce R. Kennedy

Chapter 4
Take Control of the Facts
Organize the Mountain of Academic Materials

Take control of the facts. School is a game of facts. Your job is to **RETRIEVE** the facts and **RETURN** the facts. First, you will retrieve the facts from the blackboard (class notes), handouts, and textbook, and then you will return the facts to the teacher in an essay, research paper, and on a test. You need to have an organization system in place to manage the voluminous academic facts.

For Example
Class: English
The academic facts come from 3 sources:
1. Class notes
2. Handouts
3. Textbook

For each set of facts, you will write Test Review Notes. You will now have 3 sets of Test Review Notes:
1. Class notes + Test Review Notes
2. Handouts + Test Review Notes
3. Textbook + Test Review Notes
4. Homework Assignments, Quizzes, and Tests

All Academic Materials Need to Be Organized

Test Review Notes for Class notes	Test Review Notes for Textbook

Blue Folder 1/English

Class Handouts	Test Review Notes for Handouts

Blue Folder 2/English

Homework Assignments	Quizzes and Tests

Blue Folder 3/English

Option 1. Cheap School Notebooks & Color-Coded Folders

Buy a school notebook for each class and buy color-coded folders to keep track of the following:
1. Test Review Notes (class notes, handouts, and textbook)
2. Quizzes
3. Tests
4. Homework Assignments

Buy Color-Coded Folders for Each Class:
English   Blue Folder
Math   Green Folder
Science   Yellow Folder
History   Purple Folder
Language   Red Folder

Label Your Blue Folders (3 Folders Per Class)
Folder 1. Test Review Notes
Pocket 1. Class Notes Test Review Notes
Pocket 2. Textbook Test Review Notes

Folder 2. Class Handouts
Pocket 1. Handouts
Pocket 2. Test Review Notes for Handouts

Folder 3. Homework, Quizzes, and Tests
Pocket 1. Homework Assignments
Pocket 2. Quizzes and Tests

BEFORE YOUR NEXT TEST, INVEST IN THE ACADEMIC BEST

SMARTGRADES
School Notebooks
Good Grades Become Grand Dreams

www.smartgrades.com

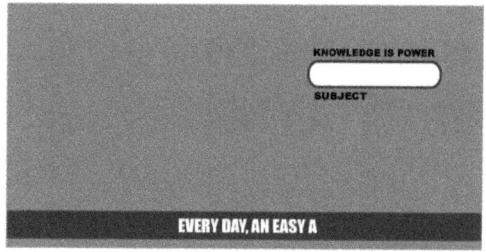

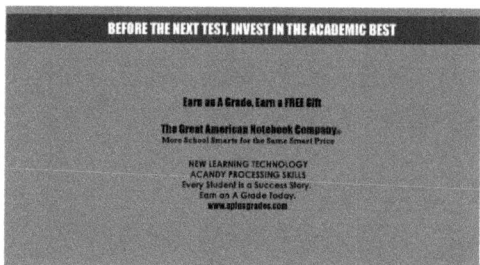

THE ESSENTIALS

Class Notes and Test-Review Notes in One Notebook
- How to Ace Every Test Every Time
- How to Ace a Multiple Choice Test
- How to Ace an Essay Test
- How to Write a Research Paper
- Homework Action Planner

BEFORE YOUR NEXT TEST, INVEST IN THE ACADEMIC BEST

Option 2. SMARTGRADES School Notebooks
You can take class notes and write Test Review Notes in the same notebook, and the new learning technology, **SMARTGRADES** Processing Tools, are at your fingertips. There is also a notebook for textbook Test Review Notes and research papers.

Homework Action Planner
SMARTGRADES Homework Action Planner to manage your life

Notebook 1. Class Notes and Test Review Notes
SMARTGRADES School Notebook for Class Notes and Test Review Notes

Notebook 2. Textbook Test Review Notes
SMARTGRADES School Notebook for Textbook Test Review Notes

Notebook 3. Research Papers
SMARTGRADES Research School Notebook to Write Papers

Handouts and Test-Review Notes
One color-coded folder for handouts and Test Review Notes

Homework, Quizzes, and Tests
One color-coded folder for homework, quizzes, and tests

SMARTGRADES Advantage:
• Buy a **SMARTGRADES** School Notebook and keep the receipt

• Earn A Grades, Earn FREE Gift!
(mail in receipt as proof-of-purchase)

• **PHOTON SUPERHERO of EDUCATION** will call you to congratulate you on your academic success.

EVERY DAY AN EASY A

How to Organize Your Study Area

Tools of the Trade

Choose a Great Study Area
Choose a Power Study Snack
Design a Study Schedule
Choose a School Library Locker

Steps to Success

Right after class, you will immediately go to your favorite study area and write your Test Review Notes. You will read your class notes, handout, and textbook and use your ten step **SMARTGRADES** Processing Tools for Instant & Total Recall to ace your tests (Chapter 7).

How to Choose a Great Study Area

- ☐ 1. Choose study area with no external distractions
- ☐ 2. Spacious desk for notebook, textbook, and reference materials
- ☐ 3. Comfortable chair that fits your body type
- ☐ 4. Good lighting
- ☐ 5. Computer with internet connection, printer, ink, and paper
- ☐ 6. External hard drive for daily backups of schoolwork
- ☐ 7. Pens, pencils, stapler, tape, paper clips, and ruler

How to Choose a Power Study Snack

Learning requires a great deal of energy. Every two hours, you will need some nutrition. When you are hungry, you will start searching for food. You will waste a lot of time walking up and down the aisles of a supermarket, and will be tempted as a result of persuasive advertisements to choose some processed food in a plastic wrapper that is loaded with sugar and salt and is devoid of vitamins and minerals. Or you will succumb to eating greasy junk food that will leave you undernourished and fat.

On one hand, you may need that walk to stretch your legs and get some fresh air. On the other hand, there are too many temptations, and you will waste too much time and spend more money than your budget allows.

Make a Daily Power Study Snack Plan:
M: Yogurt, granola, and fruit
T: Bran muffin in a variety of flavors
W: Turkey sandwich with red peppers and cheese
TH: Carrots and celery sticks with humus
F: Trail Mix: Almonds, walnuts, cranberries, raisins
- Always carry a bottle of water with you to stay hydrated.
- Avoid soft drinks loaded with sugar that make you fat.

How to Design a Study Schedule

The ideal study schedule has 45-Minute study periods and 15-Minute breaks.

Example
4-4:45 p.m.
Math Homework
45 Minutes
15 Minute Break: Stretch, Eat a Study Snack, Drink Water

5-5:45 p.m.
Science Homework
45 Minutes
15 Minute Break: Stretch, Eat a Study Snack, Drink Water

6-6:45 p.m.
English Homework
45 Minutes
15 Minute Break: Stretch, Eat a Study Snack, Drink Water

The Study Rules:
- If you have a test the next day, do your test preparation before you tackle your homework because test preparation takes more time and energy.
  Example:
  Priority # 1 English Test Tomorrow
  Priority # 2 Science Report Due Friday

- Do your math homework before you do your other assignments because math takes more time and energy.
  Example:
  Priority # 1 Math Problems
  Priority # 2 English Essay (Ask parent to proofread paper)

How to Choose a School Library Locker

Lugging heavy textbooks is bad for your back and posture.

Q: Are you starting to slouch?

Some schools have lockers in the library. This is a great place for a locker because you can leave your heavy textbooks in your locker and study in the library. You won't have to carry heavy books back and forth from the library. You will also be able to place your supplementary library books into your locker.

First Come, First Serve
The top lockers are reserved early and first. If you wait too long to buy a library locker, you will have to buy a bottom locker that is adjacent to your knees.

DAILY ACTION PLAN

- [ ] 1. Call school library and ask if there are library lockers.
- [ ] 2. Go to the library and examine the lockers.
- [ ] 3. Add your **SMARTGRADES** School Notebooks and textbooks to your locker. You can also add your gym clothes.
- [ ] 4. Checkout supplementary textbooks that will help you learn the academic materials, and add to locker.
- [ ] 5. Do your homework in the school library and leave your heavy schoolbooks in the library locker.

PHOTON'S
Spiritual Illuminations
8 Superpowers of Stress-Relief

1. RECOGNIZE Your Star Qualities.

2. LISTEN to Your Inner Voice.

3. PROTECT Your Needs and Desires.

4. Have COURAGE to Abandon Relationships with insensitive people.

5. Attach Your HEART to Your HEAD and Make Decisions in Your Best Interest.

6. EMPOWER Yourself to Make the Necessary Changes to Ensure Your Happiness.

7. Have the VISION to See Beyond Present Difficulties and Create a Stress-Free Lifestyle.

8. Take Good Care of Yourself, You Belong to You

PHOTON
SUPERHERO OF EDUCATION
www.BooksnotBombs.com

SMART POWER IS BACK IN THE HANDS OF ALL STUDENTS

Chapter 5
Manage Your Worry, Anxiety, Stress, and Bouts of Depression

If You Learn Anything at Cornell,
Please Learn to Ask for Help.
It Is a Sign of Wisdom and Strength!

David Skorton
President of Cornell University
(2010: 6 Suicides in 6 Months)

Chapter 5
Manage Your Worry, Anxiety, Stress, and Bouts of Depression

Here are some of the reasons that most, if not all, students are anxious, stressed, and suffer "bouts of depression."

1. **Poor Time Management Tools:** Time cannot be saved. Students do not know how to take control of their time to make every hour count toward reaching their academic goals (Chapter 1 and 2).

2. **Disorganization:** The academic facts are voluminous (class notes, handouts, and textbook) and students do not have an organization system in place to manage the mountain of facts (Chapter 4).

3. **Energy Is Scattered in Too Many Directions:** Students are over scheduled. KEEP LIFE SIMPLE. Stick to your priorities of class, study period, part-time job, and exercise. Limit yourself to one or two activities a week, e.g., sporting event, music concert, or film.

4. **No Energy to Learn:** Students eat fast food, junk food and processed food devoid of nutrition (Chapter 3).

5. **Poor Processing Tools:** Students wait until the night before a test to start memorizing academic material. Students do not have learning tools to process the facts for long-term retention to ace their tests (Chapter 7).

6. **Friendship Stress:** Students are trying to form a relationship of mutual affection and admiration. Bonding your soul with the soul of another person for companionship is a challenging undertaking because both of you are still maturing and don't have defined identities. As a result, relationships are fragile. All breakups are painful to one degree or another.

7. **Worry, Anxiety, and Stress Can Escalate into Depression and Suicide:** Students feel overwhelmed by the demands of school, work, part-time jobs, and relationships (family and friends). When disappointments build up, so does the emotional pain. The emotional pain can be too much to bear and depression will take hold of your soul and immobilize you, until the problems can be resolved.

LIFE IS UNFAIR
Everything Under the Sun Has a Short Lifespan and an Expiration Date.

Disappointments Multiply –>
Emotional Pain Is Too Much To Bear –>
Pain –> Rage –> Depression –>Suicide

For Example: This Student Is Having a Bad Week

1. Unfair Tricky Test Questions –> Emotional Pain
A student is sabotaged by unfair tricky test questions from a teacher with an ax to grind. You paid your tuition, studied for hours, and the entire class fails the test and it is graded on a curve. This teacher is undermining your self-confidence, destroying your self-esteem, and your dream for the future.

2. Illness or Death in the Family —> Emotional Pain
The doctor did not diagnose the symptoms in time and now it is too late to help your family member. The bad news has broken your heart. Family members cannot be replaced. Grieving the loss of a loved one takes at least three years.

3. Your Friend Breaks Up with You –> Emotional Pain
Your friend is no longer interested in hanging out with you. This pain takes time to heal. After a few months, you will feel better and be able to make new friends.

4. Your Beloved Pet Dies –> Emotional Pain
You pet passes away from old age. Even though no one gets to live forever and your pet had a great life, the loss of your pet hurts deeply, your heart is broken, and you are in pain. This pain takes years to heal, but in time you will heal and be left with wonderful memories that last a lifetime.

DO NOT START POPPING THOSE VACUOUS PILLS FOR DEPRESSION

WHY?

Because all medications have side effects and you will find that you will now be suffering from your emotional pain and from the side effects of these medications. These pills are also dangerous because when you feel emotional pain, you keep popping the pills, like candy, overdose, and die. Prescription drugs are more dangerous than illegal drugs. These pills mask your emotional pain, and will not help you to grieve your losses and heal.

FEEL TO HEAL

When you feel pain, go into a private area and cry out your emotional pain and grief for hours, weeks, days, or years. The loss of a loved one can evoke tears for years to come, and you need to let the pain rise to the surface and be released. The day will come when the grief is over, and you will regain your vitality and zest for life.

DO NOT GIVE YOUR POWER AWAY

Do not give your power away to the people who come into your life and cause you pain. Too often, you will be caught unprepared for the changing landscape of problems that arise, sometimes from out of the blue, that make you very sad, angry, and depressed.

RED FLAGS OF DOOM AND GLOOM

Pay attention to the RED FLAGS of doom and gloom and heed their warnings. Everything in life has an expiration date.

Red Flag: Your teacher's assignments are insane. For example: Write a paper that covers the 12-18th century and examine the political, religious, cultural, and social changes that occurred. In this case, it is best to write an anonymous letter to the principal and the teacher, attach the ridiculous assignment, and let the dean and teacher work it out on their own.

Red Flag: Your friend no longer invites you over to play. For example: Your partner no longer uses the pronoun "we" with regard to going to see the new movie. It is time to let go of this relationship and find a new friend.

Red Flag: Your pet is fifteen years old. It is bittersweet. On one hand, your pet had a long and happy life, however, on the other hand, your pet is nearing the end of his/her life. You can't imagine life without your beloved furry friend who gives you unconditional love and is waiting at the door, when you return home from school to greet you. These wonderful memories will bring you joy for the rest of your life.

Let's Recap: Manage Your Anxiety, Stress and Depression
Here is the list of four stresses that are mentioned in this chapter. The first four stresses can be managed, solved, and resolved with the tools and techniques contained within this book. The fifth stress cannot be made **RIGHT** because life is **UNFAIR**. The best policy is to pay attention to the **RED FLAGS OF DOOM AND GLOOM** and change course to safer ground.

1. Time Management Tools (Chapter 1 and 2)
- Smartgrades Academic Planner (fully loaded)
- To Do List: Big Picture and Many Details
- Set Priorities: Urgent, Important, Low, Optional
- Divide and Conquer: Breakdown Big Tasks
- Use Time Logs: Estimate and Actual Time
- Prepare for Delays, Detours, and Distractions
- Manage Ten Different Types of Schedules

2. Organization: 6 Sets of Academic Facts (Chapter 2)
You will have to manage 3 sets of facts and 3 sets of Test Review Notes from each of your classes:
- Class notes and Test Review Notes (1 folder)
- Handouts and Test Review Note (2 folders)
- Textbook and Test Review Notes (1 folder)

To Do List: Get Organized for School
Option 1. Buy Cheap school notebooks and folders
Option 2. Buy **SMARTGRADES** School Notebooks (no folders)

3. Eat Right for Energy to Learn (Chapter 3)
- High Fiber Breakfast
- Power Lunch (big plate)
- Lite Dinner (small plate)
- Power Study Snacks

4. Daily Study Routine (Chapter 7)
- Eat right, sleep well, and exercise for energy to learn
- Right after class, write your Test-Review Notes
- Use the 10 Step **SMARTGRADES SUCCESS STRATEGY** for Instant & Total Recall to ace every test every time.
- Study Schedule: 45 Minute study periods and 15 Minute study breaks (stretch, hydrate, and eat study snacks)
- Do your test preparation before homework assignments

5. LIFE IS UNFAIR: Manage Worry, Anxiety, and Stress That Can Escalate into Depression and Suicide
- Pay attention to the **RED FLAGS,** the warning signs.
- Disappointments cause pain, rage, and depression.
- **LIFE IS UNFAIR.** Everything in life has an expiration date.
- Do not take prescription pills with dangerous side effects that prop you up and mask your painful feelings.
- **FEEL TO HEAL.** Grieve your losses. Let the tears roll down your face for days, weeks, or even years.
- Change course to safer ground.

SMART POWER IS BACK IN THE HANDS OF ALL STUDENT

PHOTON'S
Spiritual Illuminations

5 SUPER POWERS
TO MAKE YOUR DREAMS COME TRUE

1. TIME Is Nonrefundable
(Don't Waste Your Time)

2. ENERGY Is Rechargeable
(Set a Regular Bedtime)

3. MONEY Goes Round and Round
(You Have to Be in the Loop)

4. SELF-WORTH Is Infinite Potential
(Know Your Strengths, Iron Out Your Weaknesses)

5. LOVE Everything You Touch
(Put Your Heart into Everything)

WORLD PEACE IS COMING TO PLANET EARTH
www.BooksNotBombs.com

SMART POWER IS BACK IN THE HANDS OF ALL STUDENTS

PHOTON'S
Spiritual Illuminations

My Empowerment Affirmation

I have only one life.
My life is a valuable gift.
I am responsible for my destiny.
I changed my life to ensure my happiness.
Each day is lived fully with
purpose, enthusiasm, and joy.

WORLD PEACE IS COMING TO PLANET EARTH
www.BooksNotBombs.com

SMART POWER IS BACK IN THE HANDS OF ALL STUDENTS

Photon's Spiritual Illuminations

My Circle of Responsibility Affirmation

My Problems Have Solutions
When I Take

RESPONSIBILITY

for my problems have solutions
when I take responsibility for
my problems have solutions
when I take responsibility for
my problems have solutions
when I take responsibility for
my problems have solutions
when I take responsibility for
my problems have solutions
when I take responsibility for
my problems have solutions
when I take responsibility for
my problems have solutions
when I take responsibility for
my problems have solutions
when I take responsibility for
my problems have solutions
When I Take
RESPONSIBILITY.

WORLD PEACE IS COMING TO PLANET EARTH
www.BooksNotBombs.com

SMART POWER IS BACK IN THE HANDS OF ALL STUDENTS

Photon's Spiritual Illuminations

My Special Gifts

Inside of Me Are
SPECIAL GIFTS

I am able to use my special gifts,
If I focus on my positive qualities.

I am ready to use my special gifts,
to enhance the quality of my life.

I will use my special gifts for myself,
my loved ones, and to benefit humanity.

WORLD PEACE IS COMING TO PLANET EARTH
www.BooksNotBombs.com

He Who Asks a Question is a
Fool for Five Minutes;
He Who Does Not Ask a Question
Remains a Fool Forever!

Chinese Proverb

Chapter 6
Get the Most Out of Class

Try to Learn Something
About Everything
and Everything
About Something

Thomas Henry Huxley

Chapter 6
Get the Most Out of Class

Tools of the Trade

- Choose the Right School
- Find the Best Supplementary Textbook to Learn
- How to Preread the Textbook Chapter Before Class
- How to Pack a Well Equipped Book Bag
- How to Use Active Listening Tools
- How to Use Abbreviated Note Taking Tools
- Classroom Do's and Don'ts
- Your Teacher's Office Hours
- Emergency Student Contact Information
- Visit the School's Tutoring Center
- Nine Good Reasons to Visit Your Teacher

Steps to Success

Choose the Right School
Q. Are you in the right school? Why or Why Not?

1. _____

2. _____

3. _____

Your Supplementary Textbooks

Quite often, the assigned textbook may not be the best learning tool, and you will have to go to the bookstore and find another textbook with better illustrations that makes it easier to understand the academic material.

Q. Did you find the best supplementary textbook to help you learn the course material?

The Day Before Class

Q. Did you preread the chapter before coming to class for maximum absorption of the academic material?

2 Hours Before Class

Q. Do you have an alarm clock to wake you up early?
Q. Did you eat a nutritious meal to energize you?
Q. Do you wear a watch to keep you on time?
Q. Did you write a "Daily Action Plan"?

How to Pack a Well Equipped Book Bag

Q. Does your book bag contain the following supplies?

- ☐ 1. **SMARTGRADES** Homework Action Planner to keep track of your multiple schedules and school assignments
- ☐ 2. **SMARTGRADES** School Notebooks with learning tools at your fingertips
- ☐ 3. Pencil case filled with extra pens and pencils

☐ 4. Tissues for colds or for changing temperatures (cold to hot or hot to cold) that will give you a running nose.

☐ 5. NIVEA Lip baum for dry lips (baby blue cover is great)

☐ 6. Power Study Snacks for Energy to Learn
   a. Trail mix and water bottle to stay hydrated
   b. Oatmeal cookie, bran muffin
   c. Apple, apricots, or dates
   d. Turkey sandwich on whole grain bread

☐ 7. Tape Recorder to Capture Lecture Notes

There are days when you will go to class and feel tired. You didn't sleep well or eat right and have low energy. Or you have a cold and don't feel well. This is the time to use a tape recorder to make sure you get all the facts.
1. Tape recorder, blank tape, AA or AAA batteries.
2. Right after class, go back to bed and take a nap.

In Class: How to Choose the Right Seat

Q. Are you sitting in a desk where you can clearly see the blackboard and hear your teacher's lecture?

Q. Are you sitting next to friends who talk during a lecture?

Q. Are you sitting too close to the noisy air conditioner, hallway, door (opens and closes), or window (street noise)?

Your Teacher's Office Hours *

Q. Do you have your teacher's office hours and phone number?

Class:
Teacher's Name::
Office Address:
Teacher's Office Hours:
Teacher's Office Phone Number:
Teacher's E-mail Address:

The Phone Number of a Study Buddy *

Do you have an emergency phone number of a student in each of your classes in case you don't feel well and can't come to class?

Class:
Student's Name:
Student's Phone Number:
Student's E-mail Address:

* A **SMARTGRADES** School Notebook contains a built-in directory to record this information, and has 1000 learning tools at your fingertips.

Asking Questions in Class

Ask your teacher what he/she prefers. Should you raise your hand during a lecture, ask your questions at the end of the lecture, or go to the office after class and ask your question. Whatever the case, write down the questions so you don't forget them.

Example:

Q. "With all due respect, I am confused and in need of clarification of ....?"

My School's Tutoring Center

If you are having difficulty understanding a lesson, go directly to the tutoring center for academic help.

Visit Tutoring Center:

Q. What is the phone number of the tutoring center?

Q. What is the director's name?

Q. Where is the tutoring center located?

Q. When is it open?

Q. Do you have to make an appointment or can you walk-in?

My Private Learning Specialist

If you can afford private tutoring sessions, set up your sessions as soon as possible because your tutor may not be available when you are in need of assistance.

Steps to Success

Step 1. Preread Your Textbook Chapter Before Class
If you preread the textbook chapter before class, all of the academic material will be familiar, and you will have a higher level of absorption and greater understanding.

Step 2. Practice Active Listening During Class
According to research studies, we remember a dismal 25-50% of what we hear. Listening is therefore a skill that we can all benefit from improving. The way to become a better listener is to practice "active listening" as follows:

- ☑ Sit at a desk where you can clearly see and hear the teacher.

- ☑ Look at the teacher directly, nod, and smile.

- ☑ Clear your mind of all internal distractions.

- ☑ If internal thoughts interfere, write them down and deal with them later. If you are hungry, you will not be able to ignore your hunger pain, so make sure you eat something with fiber (no cravings) before class, e.g., bran muffin.

- ☑ Ignore all external distractions, e.g., cellphone.

- ☑ Stop forming counter arguments while the other person is speaking.

Step 3: Use Active Note-Taking Skills During Class
When you take notes, restate a message with fewer words, and locate the main point.

Topic:
Main Ideas:
Supporting Examples, Evidence, Explanations:

Step 4: Use Abbreviations to Take Quick Notes

For example = e.g.

Step 5: Use a Tape Recorder to Record the Lecture
A tape recorder allows you to spend more time listening and learning and less time stressing out over note taking.

Step 6: Ask Questions in Class

Seek clarification by asking a question:

Q. "What do you mean when you say..."

Step 7: Ask Questions About Test
When the teacher gives you a date for the test, ask questions about the test, such as:
Q. What is the format of the test?
Q. How many questions are on the test?
Q. What topics are covered? What is not covered?
Q. How does the test count toward percentage of grade?
Q. How is test scored? Is there a penalty for guessing?
Q. Are there sample exams on file in the library?
Q. Is the test cumulative?

Step 8: Write Down the Homework Assignment
Don't memorize the homework assignment, write it down in your Smartgrades Academic Planner, and check it twice for accuracy.

How to Preread a Textbook Chapter

Before class, preread the textbook chapter to increase your understanding and absorption of the academic material.

Step 1. Read the End-of-Chapter Summary
Read the end-of-chapter summary for an overview of the main points of the chapter.

Step 2. Read the Boldface Headings of the Chapter
Read for a general overview of the material of the chapter. Read the boldface headings and subheadings. Read actively with a pencil/highlighter in hand and write down the main idea and major and minor points of the chapter.

Main Idea:

Major Points:
1.
2.
3.

Minor Points:
1.
2.
3.

After Class Read Textbook for In-Depth Comprehension
After class, you will go back to your class notes, handouts, and textbook and read for in-depth comprehension and write Test Review Notes. You will use your, **SMARTGRADES SUCCESS STRATEGY**, to process academic material for Instant & Total Recall to ace your exams (Chapter 7).

Your Teacher's Office Hours

Here are nine very good reasons to visit your teacher:

☑ Visit 1: Introduction
Visit your teacher to introduce yourself.

☑ Visit 2: Seek Clarification
Visit your teacher to ask a question.

☑ Visit 3: Approval of Topic and Outline of Paper
Visit your teacher for approval of topic and outline of your paper.

☑ Visit 4: Approval of Rough Draft of Paper
Visit your teacher for approval of rough draft of your paper.

☑ Visit 5: Teacher's Comments
Visit your teacher to discuss comments on your paper.

☑ Visit 6: Unfair Test Question
Visit your teacher to complain about an unfair test question.

☑ Visit 7: Grading Error
Visit your teacher to complain about a grading error.

☑ Visit 8: Express Gratitude
Visit your teacher to say thank you to express your appreciation for a great class.

☑ Visit 9: Recommendation for Your Resume
Visit your teacher to ask for a recommendation to accompany your resume.

Classroom Do's

1. Do come to class prepared, having completed the reading assignments.

2. Do come to class with energy to learn: Nutritious breakfast, sufficient sleep, and daily exercise.

3. Do show up on time for class.

4. Do sit in the front rows of the classroom.

5. Do come to class with proper school supplies: Pens, pencils, sharpener, eraser, textbook, Smartgrades School Notebooks and Academic Planner.

6. Do develop a positive mental attitude about school and your goals.

7. Do your best to be sure that your work is done to your best ability, and within deadlines.

8. Do let the teacher know when you must miss class or an exam in advance, whenever possible.

9. Do ask questions in class when you do not understand the teacher's explanation.

Classroom Don'ts

1. Don't walk in or out of class while the class is in session to go to the bathroom or answer a cellphone.

2. Don't overparticipate in class discussions. Give others a chance to contribute to the discussion.

3. Don't call your teacher at home unless you have permission to do so.

4. Don't leave class early. This is disruptive and rude.

5. Don't correct the teacher in front of the class.

6. Don't have side conversations with students during class.

7. If you have a question, ask the teacher, not another student, or you will both be lost.

8. Don't act disinterested, pompous, or bored during class.

9. Every class is important. If you are absent from class, don't ask your teacher if you missed anything important.

10. If you have a problem it is best to see the teacher first, if possible. Don't go over the teacher's head unless you have to.

11. Don't sit in the last seat in the backrow of the classroom when there are empty seats available up front.

Let's Recap: How to Get the Most Out of Class

1. Preread Textbook Chapter
   Q. Did you preread the textbook chapter for maximum absorption of the academic material?

2. Eat Right for Energy to Learn
   Q. Did you eat a high fiber breakfast before class?

3. Choose the Right Seat
   Q. Did you choose a seat where you can see and hear?

4. Active Listening Skills
   Q. Did you learn how to focus your attention to avoid external and internal distractions?

5. Active Note Taking Skills
   Q. Did you locate the main ideas and supporting details?

6. Abbreviation Skills
   Q. Did you abbreviate repetitive words?

7. Asking Questions in Class
   Q. Did you ask a question to clarify confusion?

8. Asking Questions About the Test
   1. Did you ask about the kind of test?
   2. Are there sample exams filed in the library?
   3. How is the test scored?

9. Homework Assignment Skills
   Q1. Did you write down the homework assignment in a Smartgrades Academic Planner (not in your head or on a piece of scrap paper)?

   Q2. Did you check the assignment twice for accuracy?

The More You Understand,
The Less You Have to Remember.

Craig A. McCraw

In 24 Hours, F Students Become A Students

Sharon Rose Sugar
The Paladin of Education for the 21st Century

THIS BOOK SAVES LIVES
"The Silent Crisis Destroying America's Brightest Minds"
"Book of the Month" Alma Public Library, Wisconsin

Chapter 7
SMARTGRADES
PROCESSING TOOLS
ACE EVERY TEST EVERY TIME

10 STEP SMARTGRADES PROCESSING TOOLS

    Step 1.   Estimation Tool
    Step 2.   Divide and Conquer Tool
    Step 3.   Active Reading Tool
    Step 4.   Extraction Tool
    Step 5.   Condensation Tool
    Step 6.   Association Tool
    Step 7.   Test Review Note Tool
    Step 8.   Conversion Tool
    Step 9.   Visualization Tool
    Step 10. Self Test Tool

In-Depth Comprehension
Long-Term Retention
Mastery of the Material

Chapter 7
SMARTGRADES PROCESSING TOOLS
ACE EVERY TEST EVERY TIME
Process Facts for Instant & Total Recall

Are You Test Ready?

Education is food for the brain. Students spend the entire day eating facts and building their brain muscles. If I give you a sandwich to eat, you cannot stuff the entire sandwich into your mouth. You have to take small bites and chew, chew, chew, and digest. Eating facts is like eating a sandwich. You have to take small amounts of information and chew (in-depth comprehension), chew (long-term retention), and chew (mastery of academic material).

Right after every class, go directly to your study area and write your Test Review Notes for Instant & Total Recall to ace your exams.

DAILY ACTION PLAN
- ❑ 1. Get up early enough to exercise and eat breakfast
- ❑ 2. Preread the textbook chapter for maximum absorption
- ❑ 3. Go to class to receive teacher's wisdom and experience
- ❑ 4. Go to study room and write Test Review Notes for class notes, handouts, and textbook.
- ❑ 5. Use **SMARTGRADES SUCCESS STRATEGY** to process facts for Instant & Total Recall to ace every test every time.

EVERY DAY AN EASY A

SMARTGRADES SUCCESS STRATEGY

To ace your exams, you have to develop three critical skills:

RETENTION, RECOGNITION, RECALL

1. **RETENTION** is your ability to absorb the facts.
2. **RECOGNITION** is reading the test question and knowing the answer.
3. **INSTANT RECALL** is popping out an answer in a jiffy.
4. **TOTAL RECALL** is long term retention of all of the facts.

To acquire these 3 skills, you need **REVIEW** and **REPETITION**.

Here Are the 5 R's of Test Preparation
REVIEW, REPETITION, RETENTION, RECOGNITION, RECALL

The academic facts have to be processed (absorption) for Instant & Total Recall to ace your test. You have to eat facts, just like you eat food. The facts have to be digested. **SMARTGRADES SUCCESS STRATEGY** is a 10 step learning tool for Instant & Total Recall of the facts. Let's define each of the following terms:

Step 1. Estimation Tool
Step 2. Divide and Conquer Tool
Step 3. Active Reading Tool
Step 4. Extraction Tool
Step 5. Condensation Tool
Step 6. Association Tool
Step 7. Test Review Note Tool
Step 8. Conversion Tool
Step 9. Visualization Tool
Step 10. Self-Test Tool

SMARTGRADES BRAIN POWER REVOLUTION

Step 1. Estimation Tool
Every paragraph contains one main idea and many supporting details. If you have ten paragraphs, then you have ten main ideas.

Step 2. Divide and Conquer Tool
You have to process one paragraph at a time for Instant & Total Recall. You cannot stuff a whole sandwich into your mouth. You have to take small bites, chew, chew, chew, and digest.

Step 3. Active Reading Tool
When you read, you need to be holding a pencil like a fisherman holds a net over the water to capture a fish. You are fishing for the facts. Every fact is a test question.

Step 4. Extraction Tool
You job is to extract the main idea and supporting details of every paragraph: Who, What, Where, When, and Why.

Step 5. Condensation Tool
Your job is to condense the facts and make them easier to digest, absorb, and process for Instant & Total Recall.

Step 6. Association Tool
Association links the unknown fact to a known fact in your mind. This is the glue that makes the facts stick to you.

Step 7. Test Review Note Tool
Your class notes, handouts, and textbook have to be processed for Instant & Total Recall to ace your tests.

Step 8. Conversion Tool
The facts have to be converted into test questions.

Step 9. Visualization Tool
Q. What type of test question is best suited for the facts?

Step 10. Self-Testing Tool
You have to answer your test questions to make sure that you have Instant & Total Recall and can ace your tests.

EVERY DAY AN EASY A

How to Process (Absorb) the Facts to Ace a Test

Tools of the Trade

SMARTGRADES PROCESSING TOOLS
ACE EVERY TEST EVERY TIME

Steps to Success

Step 1. Gather Study Materials and Go to Study Area
- ☐ a. Class Notes
- ☐ b. Handouts
- ☐ c. Textbook

Step 2. Choose a Great Study Area
- ☐ a. No external distractions
- ☐ b. Good lighting
- ☐ c. Comfortable chair
- ☐ d. Big desk to hold all school supplies

Step 3. Clear Your Mind of All Internal Distractions
a. Worry and Anxiety: "I feel overwhelmed by workload!"
b. Fear of Failure: "I feel inadequate...I can't keep up!"
c. Negative Self-Talk: "I am not smart enough!"

Step 4. Develop Positive Self-Talk to Build Your Self-Esteem
a. "I have the power to make my dreams come true!"
b. "I have the power to transform weakness into strength!"
c. "I have the power to change bad habits into good habits!"
d. "I have the power to focus my mind on the task at hand!"

Step 5. Develop a Regular Study Period Schedule

Where do I study best:
☐ At Home ☐ In the Library ☐ Somewhere Else

When do I study best:
☐ In the Morning ☐ Afternoon ☐ Evening

How do I study best:
☐ Alone ☐ With a Friend ☐ In a Group

I need to take a break:
☐ Every 30 Minutes ☐ Every Hour ☐ Every Two Hours

Example: Weekly Study Period Schedule

M:	Study: 2-7 p.m.
T:	Study: 2-7 p.m.
W:	Study: 2-7 p.m.
TH:	Study: 2-7 p.m.
F:	Study: 10-3 p.m.
S:	Study: 12-3 p.m.
S:	Study: 1-4 p.m.

Step 6. Develop a Regular Study Period Plan with Breaks

Study for 50 minutes and then take a 10 minute study break:

2-2:50	10 minute break	Write Class Notes Test Review Notes
3-3:50	10 minute break	Write Textbook Test Review Notes
4-4:50	10 minute break	Write Handout Test Review Notes
5-5:50	10 minute break	Write Rough Draft of Paper
6-6:50	10 minute break	Do Math Homework

EVERY DAY AN EASY A

Step 7. Right After Class, Write Test Review Notes

SMARTGRADES PROCESSING TOOLS

1. Estimation Tool
How Many Main Ideas?
Every paragraph contains one main idea and many supporting details. If you have ten paragraphs, then you have ten main ideas.

Example: Estimate Main Ideas
1 main idea per paragraph
10 paragraphs = 10 main ideas

Paragraph 1
Main Idea:

Paragraph 2
Main Idea:

Paragraph 3
Main Idea:

---

2. Divide and Conquer Tool
You have to process one paragraph at a time for Instant & Total Recall. You cannot stuff a whole sandwich into your mouth. You have to take small bites, chew, chew, chew, and digest.

Paragraph 1
Main Idea:
Supporting Details:
Condense Facts:
Association Cue for Instant & Total Recall:
Possible Test Question:

SMARTGRADES BRAIN POWER REVOLUTION

115

3. Active Reading Tool

When you read, you need to be holding a pencil like a fisherman holds a net over the water to capture a fish. You are fishing for the facts. Every fact is a test question. Underline the <u>main idea</u> and <u>supporting details.</u>

Example: Underline Main Idea and Supporting Details
<u>Thomas Jefferson</u> was an intellectual, statesman, and <u>third president of the United States.</u> Although Jefferson served as <u>governor of Virginia, ambassador to France, secretary of state, vice president, and president,</u> he is remembered in history less for the offices he held than for what he stood for.

4. Extraction Tool

You job is to extract the main idea and supporting details of every paragraph: Who, What, Where, When, and Why.

Example: Extract Facts
<u>Thomas Jefferson</u> was an intellectual, statesman, and <u>third president of the United States.</u> Although Jefferson served as <u>governor of Virginia, ambassador to France, secretary of state, vice president, and president,</u> he is remembered in history less for the offices he held than for what he stood for.

    One Main Idea   Many Supporting Details

Main Idea: Thomas Jefferson, 3rd President of U.S.A.

Many Supporting Details:
- Held many offices
- President
- Vice President
- Ambassador
- Secretary of State

5. Condensation Tool
Your job is to condense the facts and make them easier to digest, absorb, and process for Instant & Total Recall.

Many Supporting Details:
- Held many offices
- President
- Vice President
- Ambassador
- Secretary of State

Example:Condense Facts
Held Many Offices = P/VP/AM/SS

6. Association Tool for Instant & Total Recall
Association links the unknown fact to a known fact in your mind. Choose the Association Cue that works best for you. Personal memory is the most powerful Association Cue.

Example: Associate Facts
P/VP/AM/SS = Association Cue = Personal Memory

My Personal Association Cue Is:
PVP played on AM radio on weekends (Sat, Sun)
Totally ridiculous memory cue, but it works for me

7. Test Review Note Tool
Your class notes, handouts, and textbook have to be processed for Instant & Total Recall to ace your tests.
- ☐ a. Test Review Note for Class Notes
- ☐ b. Test Review Note for Handouts
- ☐ c. Test Review Note for Textbook Chapter

My Test Review Note
Main Idea:
Supporting Details:
Condense Facts:
Association Cue for Instant & Total Recall:
Possible Test Question

8 & 9: Visualization and Conversion Tool
Visualize test question and convert facts, the main idea, and supporting details into a sample test question.

Q. What type of test question is best suited for the facts?

Sample Test Question
Q. What positions did Thomas Jefferson hold?
(a) 3rd President of U.S.A.
(b) Governor of Virginia
(c) Ambassador to France
(d) Secretary of State U.S.A.
(e) Vice President of U.S.A.
(g) All of the Above

10. Self-Testing Tool for Instant & Total Recall
To ace a test, you need to process (absorb) the facts for long-term retention. Cramming facts for short-term retention does not work because you won't have Instant & Total Recall to ace your tests.

Q. Can you recall the facts in a jiffy for Instant Recall?
Q. Can you recall all of the facts for Total Recall?

If you can't remember the fact, change the association cue.

Use SMARTGRADES Processing Tools to Write Test Review Notes
Time Log
Estimate: 5 Hours
Actual:
Error:
Speedbumps: Delays, Detours, or Distractions?

How to Associate Facts for Instant & Total Recall

The facts have to be processed for Instant & Total Recall to ace your test. To process the facts for long-term retention, you have to link the **UNKNOWN** fact to a **KNOWN** fact in your mind. This linking process is called **ASSOCIATION**. For example, here are two unknown words:

Yin   Yan**g**

One of these words is male and the other word is female. The word Yan**g** is male. To process the fact for Instant & Total Recall, we want to associate the fact, that is link the **unknown** fact to a **known** fact in our mind.

	Association	
Unknown Fact	LINK	**Known** Fact in Mind
Yan**g** (male)	LINK	"g looks like a penis"

The letter "g' on the Yan**g** looks like a male penis. You will remember this fact in an Instant and you will remember this for a lifetime. We linked the **unknown** fact to a **known** fact in your mind. This is how to achieve **Instant & Total Recall** of the facts.

Steps to Success

Step 1. Selection
Select facts to memorize: Main ideas and Supporting Details (who, what, where, when why, and how).

Step 2. Association
Choose the association cue that fits your learning style.

Acronym Cue: Use letters to condense the key facts. For example, to remember how to shoot a rifle, use the classic acronym BRASS, which stands for: Breath, Relax, Aim, Sight, Squeeze.

Acrostic Cue: Use a sentence to condense the key facts. For example, to remember the order of G-clef notes on sheet music, (E, G, B, D, F) use the classic acrostic: Every Good Boy Deserves Fun.

Rhyme Cue: Use rhymes to link the key facts together. For example, the classic, "I before E, except after C."

Music Cue: Make up a song or poem with the information in it. Sing the song or recite the poem several times.

Chaining Cue: Create a story where each word or idea you have to remember cues the next idea you need to recall. Use your imagination. If you had to remember the name, Shirley Temple, you could rhyme Shirley with curly and remember that she had curly hair around her temples.

Funny Cue: Write a joke that contains the key facts. The funniest, most outlandish, and the strangest concoction of memory cues makes memorizing easy.

EVERY DAY AN EASY A

10 Step SMARTGRADES PROCESSING TOOLS

My Test Review Notes to Ace the Test

Paragraph 1
• Extract Facts:
Main Idea:
Supporting Details:
a.
b.
c.

• Condense Facts:

• Associate Facts:

• Convert to Test Question:
Q. Who, What, Where, When, Why, How?

• Self-Test for Instant and Total Recall

Paragraph 2
• Extract Facts:
Main Idea:
Supporting Details:
a.
b.
c.

• Condense Facts:

• Associate Facts:

• Convert to Test Question:
Q. Who, What, Where, When, Why, How?

• Self-Test for Instant and Total Recall

Paragraph 3
• Extract Facts:
Main Idea:
Supporting Details:
a.
b.
c.

• Condense Facts:

• Associate Facts:

• Convert to Test Question:
Q. Who, What, Where, When, Why, How?

• Self-Test for Instant and Total Recall

Paragraph 4
• Extract Facts:
Main Idea:
Supporting Details:
a.
b.
c.

• Condense Facts:

• Associate Facts:

• Convert to Test Question:
Q. Who, What, Where, When, Why, How?

• Self-Test for Instant and Total Recall

How to Develop a Study Group

Study groups can keep you and your friends on track for academic success. These groups help everyone because they facilitate the learning process by thinking out loud, sharing ideas, and learning from each other.

There are many benefits to forming a study group:
1. Improves your understanding of the material
2. Share your talents
3. Provides an emotional support system to motivate you
4. Learning can be drudgery and sharing the tedious task lessens the pain.

Tools of the Trade

How many students?
Who should be in the study group?
Where should you hold the study sessions?
How long should a study session be?
When should the study group meet?
Who is the leader of the group?
What are the objectives and goals?

Steps to Success

Step 1. How Many Students?
The best size for a study group is four to six people. Small groups don't have man power to get things done. Large groups are harder to manage.

Step 2. Who Are the Members?

The best study groups are composed of individuals who share the same interest in doing well in class and on tests. Everyone has different strengths and weakness. By participating in a study group you are able to benefit from the talents of other group members.

Step 3. Where Do We Meet?

Study group sessions should be held in a location where you can talk and bring your power study snacks. The best place is an empty classroom, office space or dining room table.

Step 4. How Long Do We Study?

Study group sessions should be not longer than two to three hours. If the study session is too short, you can't accomplish anything. If it is too long, you loose interest and focus. Its best to schedule breaks every 45 minutes for a ten minute study snack.

Step 5. When Do We Meet?

Try to meet at the same time and place each week. Creating a set routine will help each member to plan ahead and come prepare to each session.

Step 6. Who Is the Leader of the Group?

Each group study session should have a leader. It's the leaders responsibility to make sure that the group is focused and stays on track.

Step 7. What Are the Objectives of the Study Group?

Doing well in school is all about retrieving the facts from your class notes, handouts and textbook reading assignments, and then returning the facts on a test. The facts have to processed (absorbed) for Instant & Total Recall to ace your tests.

Each member can contribute their own particular strength to the group. Instead of one student doing all of the study tasks, they can be divided up among the study group. It is best to make a list of the tasks and divide and conquer, as follows:

Example: Divide Up Academic Tasks Among Members
1. One member takes copious notes in class.

2. One member collates the best supplementary reading materials to further a deeper understanding of the material.

3. One member has a good reparte with the teacher, visits the office once a week, and has a crystal clear understanding of the teacher's expectations.

4. One member collates old exams for practice test questions.

5. One member prepares power study snacks.

6. Three members divide up writing Test Review Notes
    a. Class Notes Test Review Notes
    b. Handouts Test Review Notes
    c. Textbook Test Review Notes

7. One member prereads the chapter, takes notes, and hands them out an hour before class.

What Is Your Learning Style

How to Understand Your Learning Style

Identifying and understanding your learning style is critical to your study preparation. By knowing how you learn best you can select a school, class, teacher, textbook, and ultimately a career that appeals to your unique way of learning things.

Tools of the Trade

Visual (most common)
Auditory (languages, music)
Tactile (kinesthetic)
Logical (mathematical)
Social (interpersonal)

Steps to Success

Read definitions below to figure out how you learn best.

Visual Learning Style
Students learn best when ideas or subjects are presented in a visual format, with pictures, diagrams, videos or overhead projectors.

Auditory Learning Style
Students are able to learn, understand and retain information better when they hear it rather than see it. Students learn by participating in class discussion, by listening to a teacher lecture, or listening to audio tapes. For example, students who excel at learning languages and composing music are auditory learners.

Tactile Learning Style
Tactile learners are hands-on learners. They learn by touching and feeling. They learn best when they are able to physically participate directly in what they are required to learn or understand. For example, students who excel at work which requires hands-on skills, such as dentistry, surgery or carpentry.

Solitary Learning Style
Students who are private, introspective and independent. They are able to concentrate and focus on a specific project without outside help. Solitary learners prefer to work on problems in isolation. For example, writers, scientists, and entrepreneurs are solitary learners.

Logical Learning Style
Students who prefer to use their brain for logical and mathematical reasoning prefer the logical learning style. Logical learners can recognize patterns easily and are good at making logical connections between what would appear to most people to be meaningless content.

Social Learning Style

Students who communicate well will others, both verbally and non-verbally. Social learners prefer learning in groups or classes and typically like to spend one-on-one time with a teacher or an instructor. For example, teachers and therapists are good listeners and are able to understand other's views.

1. What is your learning style?

2. How does understanding your learning style help you to make informed choices about your destiny?

3. Do you now understand why you would rather go to your room and write a book or become a teacher and work with a group, rather than work with your hands and become a dentist, like your father?

4. What career choices fit your learning style best?

PHOTON'S
INTRODUCTION TO WRITING
WORLD PREMIERE!
Writing Is an Art Form

10 Esoteric Laws of Genius and Creativity (Chapter 11)
1. VESSEL
2. INSPIRATION
3. IMPREGNATION
4. INCUBATION
5. GENESIS
6. SILENT: LISTEN
7. METAPHORPHOSIS
8. REVELATION
9. SIGNATURE
10. IMMORTALITY

How to Write a School Paper
- Research Topic (Chapter 8)
- Choose a Researchable Topic
- Find Experts in Field
- Use Direct and Indirect Quotes
- Read Primary Source Material
- List Pro and Con Arguments
- Paraphrase Facts (in your own words)
- Apply Critical Thinking Tools (Chapter 10)
- Outline Main Ideas and Supporting Details
- Writing is Rewriting: Rough Draft to Final Draft

Use Standard Paper Organization:
Introduction, Body, and Conclusion

Use Standard Paragraph Organization:
5 Sentences: Intro, Quote, Example, Analysis, Conclusion

Use Transition Words to Bridge Ideas:
According to, For example, As a result, In conclusion,

Add Citations: Footnotes or Endnotes
Add Bibliography

Proofread Paper to Perfection (Chapter 9)
Grammar, Spelling, Punctuation, Neatness

There's No Such Thing
As Good Writing.
There's Only Good Rewriting.

Mark Twain

Chapter 8, Part I
Read, Write, and Proofread

English Essays
Research Papers

English is a unique language. Why is the word phonetic not spelled the way it sounds? There's no egg in eggplant, no ham in hamburger, neither apple nor pine in pineapple. English muffins weren't invented in England nor French fries in France. Quicksand can work slowly, boxing rings are square, and a guinea pig is neither from Guinea, nor is it a pig. The plural of tooth is teeth, so why isn't the plural of booth beeth? If you wrote a letter, perhaps you bote your tongue? People recite at a play, and play at a recital; ship by truck, and send cargo by ship; have noses that run, and feet that smell; park on driveways, and drive on parkways. A slim chance and a fat chance mean the same, but a wise man and a wise guy are opposites. Overlook and oversee are opposites, while quite a lot and quite a few are alike. A house can burn up as it burns down, a form can be filled in by being filled out, an alarm clock goes off by going on. On the other hand, so to speak, some things are talked about only when they are absent; i.e., we do not hear about a horseful carriage or a strapful gown, a sung hero or required love, someone who is combobulated, gruntled, ruly, or peccable.

Unknown Internet Quote

Chapter 8
Write an A Grade Paper

Tools of the Trade

Research Topic
Choose Researchable Topic
Use Library Databases
Use Encyclopedia for General Overview
Find Experts in Field
Read Primary Sources (autobiographical)
Read Secondary Sources (biographical)
List Pro and Con Arguments
Paraphrase Research (in your own words)
Use Direct and Indirect Quotes
Document Source Material: MLA, APA, Chicago Style

Write Paper
Write Outline
Write Thesis Statement
Use Standard Paper Structure
Use Standard Paragraph Structure
Use Transition Words to Bridge Paragraphs and Ideas
Apply Critical Thinking Tools (Chapter 10)
Seek Teacher's Approval for Outline and Rough Drat
Write Final Draft
Add Citations: Footnotes or Endnotes
Add Bibliography
Proofread Paper to Perfection (Chapter 9)

There Are Four Basic Types of Essays:
Description, Narration, Exposition, Persuasion

Each of these types of essays has its distinctive characteristics; however, you will find that essays are often a combination of the various forms.

1. Expository
2. Descriptive
3. Explanatory
4. Illustrative
5. Analytical
6. Argumentative
7. Defining
8. Evaluative
9. Interpretive

Definitions of Essays

1. **Expository:** An essay to convey "information."

2. **Descriptive:** An essay that describes something or someone, a situation or a location.

3. **Explanatory:** An essay that looks for reasons or causes in relation to perceived effects or results based on theory.

4. **Illustrative:** An essay that is fairly descriptive, but illustrations need to be relevant and appropriate, and written with explicit reference to the theoretical point being supported.

5. **Analytical:** An essay for experimental data. It is the process of breaking down something into its component parts, often in order to analyse patterns or categories based on a theoretical position.

6. **Argumentative:** An essay of debate and disagreement.

7. **Defining:** An essay based on a definition of terms.

8. **Evaluative:** An essay that requires you to pass judgement or make an assessment, according to stated criteria.

9. **Interpretive:** An essay where your interpretation is examined in the context of other more established interpretations.

EVERY DAY AN EASY A

A Simple Overview of Essay Paper

Steps to Success

Step 1. Restatement of Essay Question
Read essay question and restate question as the topic sentence of essay.

Here is a sample essay question:
Q. If your doctor told you that you had only a few months to live, how would you alter your way of life? Discuss.

To answer this essay question, first restate the question as the introductory sentence of your essay, as follows:
If (my) doctor told (me) that (I) had only a few months to live, (I) would alter (my) way of life by... add on the facts.

Step 2. Write Outline of Essay to Organize Thoughts
Write outline of main ideas and supporting examples.

Essay Outline
Main Idea 1. Spend more time with loved ones
Supporting Example: Take pictures for a lasting legacy

Main Idea 2. Visit the beautiful places on earth
Supporting Example: Take a trip to Hawaii

Step 3. Use Standard Essay and Paragraph Structure

Use standard essay structure: Introduction, Body, and Conclusion.

Introduction	Introduce Topic Introduce Main Ideas 1, 2, and 3˙
Body	Paragraph 1 Introduce Main Idea 1 Add: Supporting Example Add: Direct or Indirect Quote Add: Analysis, Critical Thinking Tools Add: Concluding Sentence Add: Transition Words to Link Ideas
Body	Paragraph 2 Introduce Main Idea 2 Add: Supporting Example Add: Direct or Indirect Quote Add: Analysis, Critical Thinking Tools Add: Concluding Sentence Add: Transition Words to Link Ideas
Body	Paragraph 3 Introduce Main Idea 3 Add: Supporting Example Add: Direct or Indirect Quote Add: Analysis, Critical Thinking Tools Add: Concluding Sentence Add: Transition Words to Link Ideas
Conclusion	Restate Introduction and Main Ideas Sum it all up

Step 1. Research Topic

Tools of the Trade

How to Use Library Databases
Use Encyclopedia for General Overview of Topic
List Experts in Field
List Pro and Con Arguments
Read Primary Sources (Autobiographical)
Read Secondary Sources (Biographical)
Document Sources: MLA, APA, Chicago Style
Paraphrase Don't Plagiarize
Organize: Smartgrades Research School Notebook
Take Control of Your Time with Time Logs

Steps to Success

Step 1. Use Encyclopedia for General Overview of Topic
Q. Who are the experts in the field?
   1. Expert:

   2. Expert:

   3. Expert:

Step 2. Read Bibliographic Notes for a List of Primary and Secondary Source Materials on the Topic

Q. How many source materials are required for paper?

1. Primary Source (autobiographical):
Book:
Author:
Publisher:
Copyright:
Page #

2. Primary Source (autobiographical):
   Book:
   Author:
   Publisher:
   Copyright:
   Page #

3. Secondary Source (biographical):
   Book:
   Author:
   Publisher:
   Copyright:
   Page #

Step 3. Read Primary and Secondary Source Materials for Pro and Con Arguments and Quotes (Direct and Indirect).

Expert in Field:
Pro Argument:
Direct or Indirect Quote:
Citation: Book, Author, Publisher, Copyright, Page #

Expert in Field:
Pro Argument:
Direct or Indirect Quote:
Citation: Book, Author, Publisher, Copyright, Page #

Expert in Field:
Con Argument:
Direct or Indirect Quote:
Citation: Book, Author, Publisher, Copyright, Page #

Research Topic
Time Log
Estimate Time: 10 Hours
Actual Time:
Error:
Speedbumps: Any Delays, Detours, and Distractions?

EVERY DAY AN EASY A

How to Use the Library Databases

Libraries are divided into reading rooms, restricted collections, and unrestricted book stacks.

Unrestricted Book Stacks:
- Anyone can use and read in the library, or take home

Restricted Collections:
- Special collections of rare books
- Open to Scholars, or to those with credentials

Libraries contain circulating and non-circulating materials for use only in the library, e.g., reference materials.

Step 1. Use Encyclopedia for General Overview of Topic
The leading encyclopedias are:
- Britannica
- Americana
- Collier's
- World Book

Step 2. Use Card Catalog for Primary and Secondary Sources
This is a list of all of the books in the library. The books are indexed by subject, author, and title.

Step 3. Use Newspaper Indexes for Most Recent News
Many large city newspapers provide an indexed list of all published articles.

Step 4. Use Periodical Indexes for Most Recent News
The most popular magazine articles are published in "The Readers' Guide to Periodical Literature."

Step 5. Use the Vertical File
This file contains pamphlets and brochures.

Step 6. Use the U.S. Documents Monthly Catalog
This is useful for locating government publications.

How is Your Library Organized

Most libraries use the Dewey Decimal Classification System. This system uses numbers 000-999 to classify all materials by subject matter.

The Dewey Classification System

000 - 099	General
100 - 199	Philosophy
200 - 299	Religion
300 - 399	Social Sciences
400 - 499	Language
500 - 599	Science
600 - 699	Useful Arts
700 - 799	Fine Arts
800 - 899	Literature
900 - 999	History

Library of Congress Classification System
This system uses letters to denote major categories.

A GENERAL WORKS
B PHILOSOPHY. PSYCHOLOGY. RELIGION
C AUXILIARY SCIENCES OF HISTORY
D WORLD HISTORY AND HISTORY OF EUROPE, ASIA, AFRICA, AUSTRALIA, NEW ZEALAND, ETC.
E HISTORY OF THE AMERICAS
F HISTORY OF THE AMERICAS
G GEOGRAPHY. ANTHROPOLOGY. RECREATION
H SOCIAL SCIENCES
J POLITICAL SCIENCE
L EDUCATION
M MUSIC AND BOOKS ON MUSIC
N FINE ARTS
P LANGUAGE AND LITERATURE
Q SCIENCE
R MEDICINE
S AGRICULTURE
T TECHNOLOGY
U MILITARY SCIENCE
V NAVAL SCIENCE
Z BIBLIOGRAPHY. LIBRARY SCIENCE. INFORMATION RESOURCES (GENERAL)

Library Research
Time Log
Estimate: 20 Hours (Find Books, Read Books, Take Notes)
Actual Time:
Error:

Speedbumps: Any Delays, Detours, and Distractions?

How to Write a Thesis Statement

Tools of the Trade
Researchable Topic, Question, and Point of View

What is a Thesis?
A thesis statement declares what you believe and what you intend to prove. An effective thesis has a definable, arguable claim. You must do a lot of background reading before you know enough about a subject to identify key or essential questions. You may not know how you stand on an issue until you have examined the evidence.

Steps to Success

Step 1. Select a Topic.

Example
Topic: Television sex and violence

Step 2. Ask an Interesting Question

Example
Q. What are the effects of television sex and violence on children?

Step 3. Write a Thesis Statement (Point of View)

Example: Thesis Statement
Sex and violence on television increases aggressive behavior in preschool children.

How to Paraphrase Ideas of Others
How to Write it in Your Own Words

A paraphrase is restating the ideas of others in your own words and keeping the meaning intact.

Tools of the Trade

Original Source Material
"Unique Terminology"
Main Idea and Supporting Details
Keep Meaning Intact
Add Citation: Book, Author, Publisher, Copyright, Page #

Steps to Success

Step 1. Read original passage for in-depth comprehension.

Step 2. Write down main idea and supporting ideas.

Step 3. If you used any "unique terminology" from the passage put a quote around it.

Step 4. Cite the source to credit it.

Step 5. Rewrite original passage in your own words.

Example

Original Text

Aristotle is a Greek philosopher, scientist, and educator who lived from 384 to 322 B.C. He is considered one of the greatest and most influential philosophers in Western culture. He was born in northern Greece on the Macedonian coast, in a small town called Stagira.

List Main Idea and Supporting Details:
Main Idea: Aristotle, Greek Philosopher, Scientist, Educator
Supporting Details:
(a) 384 to 322 B.C.
(b) Born: Greece, Macedonian coast, town of Stagira
    Citation: Encyclopedia

Paraphrase Text

One of the most admired and respected philosophers in Western culture was a man named Aristotle (384 to 322 B.C.). He was born in Greece in the small town of Stagira that is located on the Macedonian coast (citation: encyclopedia).

Paraphrase Source Material
Time Log
Estimate Time: 10 Hours
Actual Time:
Error:
Speedbumps: Any Delays, Detours, and Distractions?

Step 2. Write Outline of Paper

Tools of the Trade

List Experts in Field
List Pro and Con Arguments
List Arguments from Most Important to Least Important
Add Citations: Book, Author, Publisher, Copyright, Page #
Organize: Smartgrades Research School Notebook
Take Control of Your Time with Time Logs
See Teacher for Approval of Outline

Steps to Success

Step 1. Write Outline of Paper
Estimate: Pages, Paragraphs, Main Ideas
- 3 Page Paper has 3 Paragraphs Per Page
- 3 Page Paper has a Total of 9 Paragraphs
- 9 Paragraphs: 1 Main Idea Per Paragraph
- 9 Paragraphs: 7 Main Ideas Plus Intro and Conclusion

The Outline

Page 1
Paragraph 1
Write Introductory Paragraph of Paper
Write a Thesis Statement (point of view to defend).

Paragraph 2
The Most Important Main Idea Is:
Supporting Experts, Quotes, Examples, and Analysis
Citation: Book, Author, Publisher, Copyright, Page #

Paragraph 3
The Second Most Important Main Idea Is:
Supporting Experts, Quotes, Examples, and Analysis
Citation: Book, Author, Publisher, Copyright, Page #

Page 2
Paragraph 4
Main Idea:
Supporting Experts, Quotes, Examples, and Analysis
Citation: Book, Author, Publisher, Copyright, Page #

Paragraph 5
Main Idea:
Supporting Experts, Quotes, Examples, and Analysis
Citation: Book, Author, Publisher, Copyright, Page #

Paragraph 6
Main Idea:
Supporting Experts, Quotes, Examples, and Analysis
Citation: Book, Author, Publisher, Copyright, Page #

Page 3
Paragraph 7
Main Idea:
Supporting Experts, Quotes, Examples, and Analysis
Citation: Book, Author, Publisher, Copyright, Page #

Paragraph 8
Main Idea:
Supporting Experts, Quotes, Examples, and Analysis
Citation: Book, Author, Publisher, Copyright, Page #

Paragraph 9
Write the Concluding Paragraph of Paper
Restate Main Idea and Supporting Ideas and Sum It Up

The Outline
Time Log
Estimate Time: 5 Hours
Actual Time:
Error:
Speedbumps: Any Delays, Detours, and Distractions?

Step 3. Write Rough Draft of Paper

Tools of the Trade

Write a Thesis Statement
Choose Point of View and Defend Your Position

Use Standard Paper Organization:
Introduction, Body, and Conclusion

Use Standard Paragraph Organization:
Sentence 1. Introductory Sentence
Sentence 2. Expert in Field
Sentence 3. Direct or Indirect Quote
Sentence 4. Examples, Evidence, Explanations
Sentence 5. Analysis (Critical Thinking Tools)
Sentence 6. Concluding Sentence

Use Transitions to Bridge Paragraphs and Ideas
According to, For example, As a result, In conclusion

Apply Critical Thinking Tools (Chapter 10)
Separate Facts from Opinions of Author
Distinguish Theory from Reality

Add Citations: Footnotes or Endnotes
Add Bibliography
Proofread to Perfection (Chapter 9)
Take Control of Your Time with Time Logs
See Teacher for Approval of Rough Draft

Steps to Success

Step 1. Use Standard Paper Format: Introduction, Body, and Conclusion

Step 2. Write the Introduction to Your Paper
Introduce topic, supporting ideas, and include thesis statement.

For Example: Title, Topic, Introduction, Thesis Statement

"The Mountain Lion:
Once Endangered, Now a Danger

On April 23, 1994, as Barbara Schoener was jogging in the Sierra foothills of California, she was pounced on from behind by a mountain lion (Rychnovsky 39). California politicians presented voters with Proposition 197, which contained provisions repealing much of a 1990 law enacted to protect the lions."

Write a Thesis Statement: Take Point of View and Defend
"A future proposition should retain the ban on sport hunting but allow the Department of Fish and Game to control the population. Wildlife management would reduce the number of lion attacks on humans and in the long run would also protect the lions."

Step 3. Write the Body of Your Paper
Follow your Outline and introduce one main idea per paragraph followed by supporting materials of experts in field, direct and indirect quotes, evidence, and sum it up.

Step 4. Write the Conclusion of Your Paper
Restate introduction and main ideas and sum it all up.

The Rough Draft of Paper
Time Log
Estimate Time: 25 Hours
Actual Time:
Error:
Speedbumps: Any Delays, Detours, and Distractions?
Visit Teacher for Approval of Rough Draft

Use Direct and Indirect Quotes

A quotation is a reference to an authority, or a citation of an authority. There are two types of quotations: direct and indirect.

Tools of the Trade

Experts in Field
Primary and Secondary Sources
Direct Quotes
Indirect Quotes, Paraphrasing, and Transition Words
Add Citations
Short Quotation Format
Long Quotation Format

You can choose to use either type of quote. Use quotes sparingly. Always provide a context for your quotations that explains to the reader why and how the quote is relevant to the topic.

Choice 1. Direct Quotation

A direct quotation uses the exact words of an authority, and must be documented with quotation marks and a citation.

Choice 2. Indirect Quotation

An indirect quotation, or paraphrase, is a restatement of a thought expressed by someone else that is written in your own words and must be documented with a citation.

Example: Direct Quote
Author John Smith argues that "More people are dying from medical errors than from fatal diseases" (citation).

Example: Indirect Quote (Paraphrase)
According to a recent report, medical errors are killing more people than disease (citation).

Example: Combine Indirect and Direct Quotations
According to a news recent report, medical errors can be fatal as substantiated by the author John Smith, who said, "More people are dying from medical errors than from fatal diseases" (citation).

Example: Use Transition Words for Introductions
You can introduce quotations with transition words, such as, " According to…" or "In sum," as illustrated by the following:

According to Professor John Smith, "add direct quote" (citation).

Professor John Smith **sums up** the situation in the following passage: "add direct quote" (citation).

Example: Short Quotation Format

If your quotations are less than four lines long, place them in your text, and enclose them with quotation marks. This quote begins with an introductory transition word, "According to..."

According to Confucius, "Respect yourself and others will respect you" (citation).

Example: Long Quotation Format

If your quotation is more than four lines long, set it off from your text by indenting. Introduce the quotation with a complete sentence and a colon. Indent ten spaces, double space the lines, and do not use quotation marks.

Confucius sums up the situation in the following passage:

The superior man, when resting in safety, does not forget that danger may come. When in a state of security he does not forget the possibility of ruin. When all is orderly, he does not forget that disorder may come. Thus his person is not endangered, and his States and all their clans are preserved (citation).

Use Direct and Indirect Quotes with Citations
Time Log
Estimate Time: 5 Hours
Actual Time:
Error:
Speedbumps: Any Delays, Detours, and Distractions?

Use Standard Paragraph Formation

Each Paragraph in a Paper is Composed of Five Parts:

Sentence 1   Introductory Sentence and Main Idea
Sentence 2-4   Direct/Indirect Quotes from Experts
Sentence 4-6   Supporting Arguments/Examples
Sentence 6-8   Analysis (Critical Thinking Skills)
Last Sentence   Summation or Concluding Sentence

Step 1. Write the Main Idea Sentence:
According to Professor X ... (direct/indirect quote)

Step 2. Write Supporting Sentences to Defend Your Position: For example, ...

Step 3. Use Transition Words to Link Ideas
In addition, ...   Furthermore, ...   Moreover,...

Step 4. Write the Analysis Sentences:
As a result, ...
Use **SMARTGRADES** Critical Thinking Tools (Chapter 10)

Step 5. Write Concluding Sentence:
In sum, ...

Use Transition Words

Transition Words Link Ideas Within Paragraphs and Build Bridges Between Paragraphs

Transitions are words and phrases that guide a reader from one idea to the next. Use words sparingly.

To begin a sentence: However, nevertheless, furthermore, therefore

To give examples: As, for example, for instance, In other words, like, such as, that is

For causes: Accordingly, because, due to, for this, for that reason, if ...then, since

For effects: As a result, consequently, for, nevertheless, owing to, so that, therefore, so, thus

For comparisons (similarities): Along with, also, as, besides, both, furthermore, in comparison, in the same way, just as, likewise, moreover, similarly

To add an idea: Again, also, and, furthermore, equally, in addition, moreover

For contrasts (differences): Although, but, by contrast, different from, however, in contrast, instead, nevertheless, on the one hand, on the other hand, rather than, unlike, whereas, yet

For order of importance: All, best, better, first, last, least important, less important, most importantly, most of second, strongest, third, weakest

For temporal order (time): After, as soon as, before, during, finally, first, last, later, meanwhile, next, now, second, since, soon, suddenly, then, third, whenever, while, until, yesterday

For spatial order (place): Above, across, along the side, around, behind, below, beside, center, here, inside, on top of, to the left, in front of, outside, opposite, near, next to, to the center, to the right, there, where

For endings: As a result, finally, in conclusion, in summation

Use Proper Citation Style to Document Sources

Tools of the Trade

MLA Style: Writing in English and Humanities
APA Style: Writing in the Social Sciences
Chicago Style: Writing in History and Humanities

There are two reasons to document your source material:

Reason 1. Show readers where you obtained your facts.

Reason 2. Give readers a list of references should they want to read more about the subject.

Steps to Success

- Cite a source to give the origin of facts or opinions

- Cite a source when using a direct quote

- Cite a source when paraphrasing someone else's work

- Cite a source when stating an unknown fact

- Cite a source when stating controversial facts

Use Citation Format to Document Sources

Tools of the Trade

Footnotes/Endnotes
Parenthetical References

Footnotes and endnotes are basically the same thing — each provides information about where you found the material for your research paper. The only difference is where you put them in your research paper. If you use a quote from a book, you would put a footnote at the bottom (the foot) of the page that the quote appears on, citing the source of the quote. If you're using endnotes instead of footnotes, the endnote would go in a list at the end of the paper with all the other endnotes.

Example: Footnote or Endnote
1- M.I. Finley, "The Silent Women of Rome," in Horizon, no 7 (1965), Tuscaloosa, Horizon Publishers, p. 64.

Parenthetical references are brief citations, enclosed by parentheses, within the text of the paper.

Example: Parenthetical Reference
Shelley thought poets "the unacknowledged legislators of the world" (Magill 2001).

Use Endnotes, Footnotes or Parenthetical References
Time Log
Estimate Time: 5 Hours
Actual Time:
Error:
Speedbumps: Any Delays, Detours, and Distractions?

How to Write a Bibliography

Tools of the Trade

Author (last name first)
Title of Book
City: Publisher
Date of Publication

Steps to Success

1. For a Book
Author (last name first). Title of the book. City: Publisher, Date of publication.

Example:
Dahl, Roald. The BFG. New York: Farrar, Straus and Giroux, 1982.

2. For an Encyclopedia:
Encyclopedia Title, Edition Date. Volume Number, "Article Title," page numbers.

Example:
The Encyclopedia Britannica, 1997. Volume 7, "Gorillas," pp. 50-51.

3. For a Magazine:
Author (last name first), "Article Title." Name of magazine. Volume number, (Date): page numbers.

Example:
Jordan, Jennifer, "Filming at the Top of the World." Museum of Science Magazine. Volume 47, No. 1, (Winter 1998): p. 11.

4. For a Newspaper:
Author (last name first), "Article Title." Name of newspaper, city, state of publication. (date): edition if available, section, page number(s).

Example:
Powers, Ann, "New Tune for the Material Girl." The New York Times, New York, NY. (3/1/98): Atlantic Region, Section 2, p. 34.

5. For World Wide Web:
URL (Uniform Resource Locator or WWW address). author (or item's name, if mentioned), date.

Example: (Boston Globe's www address)
http://www.boston.com. Today's News, August 1, 1996.

6. For a CD-ROM:
Disc title: Version, Date. "Article title," pages if given. Publisher.

Example:
Compton's Multimedia Encyclopedia: Macintosh version, 1995. "Civil rights movement," p.3. Compton's Newsmedia.

Step 3. Write Final Draft of Paper

Tools of the Trade

Proofread Paper to Perfection (Chapter 10)

- Check Teacher's Assignment

- Check Paper Content
Q. Does Evidence Support the Thesis Statement?

- Check Paper Structure
Grammar, Spelling, Punctuation, and Neatness

- Hire a Professional Editor to Find Fatal Flaws

- Daily Back Ups on External Hard Drives

Steps to Success

Step 1. Read Assignment Again to Check Requirements
Read assignment sheet again to be sure that you understand fully what is expected of you, and that your essay/research paper meets requirements as specified by your teacher.

Step 2. Let Paper Rest and Read It with Fresh Eyes
If you let the paper sit for a few days, you will later be able to read it from a new perspective and find the remaining flaws, either in structure or content.

Step 3. SMARTGRADES Proofreading Tools (Chapter 8)
Use proofreading checklist in Chapter 8 (page 169) to correct structural or contexual errors in your paper.

Step 4. Ask a Third Party Editor to Read Your Paper
Find an online editor to read your paper and offer valuable corrections and suggestions. E-mail your paper to the professional editor, and specify a deadline that is at least two weeks before the due-date of your paper. This way, if there is a setback, you will still have time to find another editor in the nick of time to read and correct any fatal flaws.

Step 5. Print Two Copies of Your Paper
Before you hand in your paper to a teacher, make sure that you have a hard copy of your paper in case the teacher misplaces it or loses it (it happens). When your paper is returned to you, throw away your copy.

Step 6. Make Daily Back-Ups on an External Hard Drive
Make sure that you make daily back ups on an external hard drive of the work that is on your computer. There are countless horror stories of students whose computers crashed, and of research papers that were destroyed.

The Final Draft of Paper
Time Log
Estimate Time: 10 Hours
Actual Time:
Error:
Speedbumps: Any Delays, Detours, and Distractions?

EVERY DAY AN EASY A

Checklist to Write an A Grade Paper ☑

☑ **Step 1. The Essay Question**

Q. Did you answer the question asked by restating the essay question as the introductory sentence of your essay?

☑ **Step 2. Thesis Statement**

Q. Did you write a Thesis statement (defend a position)?

☑ **Step 3. Research Topic**

Q. Did you choose a researchable topic?

1. Use encyclopedia for a general overview of topic
2. Find experts in field
3. Read primary source materials (autobiographical)
4. Read secondary source materials (biographical)
5. List pro and con arguments
6. Add direct and indirect quotes from experts

☑ **Step 4. Use Critical Thinking Tools (Chapter 10)**

Q. Did you use your **SMARTGRADES** Critical Thinking Tools to separate facts from opinion of the author?

☑ **Step 5. Write Outline**

Q. Did you write an Outline of the main ideas and supporting examples to properly organize your research?

☑ **Step 6. Use Standard Paper Structure**

Q. Did you use standard paper structure: Introduction, Body, and Conclusion?

☑ **Step 7. Use Standard Paragraph Structure**

Q. Did you use standard paragraph structure: Introductory sentence, quote from expert, supporting examples, analysis, and concluding sentence?

☑ **Step 8. Paraphrase Don't Plagiarize**

Q. Did you paraphrase (write out ideas in your own words)?

☑ **Step 9. Use Transition Words**

Q. Did you use transition words to bridge paragraphs and link ideas within paragraphs? e.g., According to, For example, In addition, As a result, and In conclusion.

☑ **Step 10. Add Citations and Bibliography**

Q. Did you use citations to document your sources?

☑ **Step 11. Proofread Paper to Perfection**

Q. Did you use your **SMARTGRADES** Proofreading Tools (Chapter 8, Page 169)?

As Long as the World is Turning and Spinning, We're Gonna Be Dizzy and We're Gonna Make Mistakes.

Mel Brooks

Chapter 8, Part II
Proofread Paper to Perfection

Proofread Papers to Perfection

Tools of the Trade

Proofreading to Perfection
- ☐ Time and Patience
- ☐ Enlarging Text
- ☐ Reading Aloud
- ☐ Computer Proofreading Software, e.g., Acrobat

Proofread for Content
- ☐ Check Outline
- ☐ Check Research Material
- ☐ Check Paper Format
- ☐ Check Thesis Statement
- ☐ Check Organization of Ideas
- ☐ Check Redundancy
- ☐ Check Writing Style
- ☐ Check Facts
- ☐ Check Paraphrasing
- ☐ Check Fallacies
- ☐ Check Quotes
- ☐ Check Citation Format

Proofread for Writing Mechanics
- ☐ Check Spelling
- ☐ Check Grammar
- ☐ Check Punctuation
- ☐ Check Paragraph Format
- ☐ Check Sentences
- ☐ Check Word Usage
- ☐ Check Wordiness
- ☐ Check Clichés
- ☐ Check Word Repetition
- ☐ Check Gender
- ☐ Check 3 Nevers
- ☐ Check Neatness

Steps to Success

Step 1. Proofreading Takes Time
Proofreading is a time-intensive task. Set aside at least five to ten hours to read through your paper to proofread it to perfection.

Step 2. Enlarge Text
Your writing software allows you to enlarge the font from 12 to 22 points. You will then be able to see the smallest error, e.g., a comma that is supposed to be a period.

Step 3. Read Aloud
It is easier to find typos when you read your paper aloud. Your ears can find errors that your eyes cannot see.

Step 4. Read Aloud Computer Software
Some computers have speech software programs such as Text Edit or Adobe Acrobat software. These programs will read the paper back to you and locate writing errors.

Proofread for Writing Mechanics

Proofread for Spelling
Q. Did you use computer spellchecker to find spelling errors?

Proofread for Grammar
Q. Did you read for past, present, and future tenses?
Q. Did you keep the tenses in the present tense?

Proofread for Punctuation
Q. Did you check for capitalization of proper nouns, comma overuse, and for periods that stay inside the quotes?

Proofread for Paragraph Format
Q. Did you check for transition words, topic sentence, one main idea per paragraph, supporting examples, quote from expert in the field, analysis that uses your critical thinking skills, and concluding sentence?

Proofread for Sentences
Q. Did you check for sentence fragments, run-ons, or comma splices (change punctuation or add a conjunction).

Proofread for Word Usage
Q. Did you use the thesaurus to find the best word to communicate your ideas and express your exact meaning?

Q. Did you eliminate wordiness?

Q. Did you avoid clichés?

Proofread for Repetition
Q. Did you use the same word over and over again?

Proofread for Gender
Q. Is your use of masculine and feminine pronouns like "he" or "she" appropriate?

Proofread for 3 Nevers
Never begin a sentence with "and" or "because."
Never include personal opinions.
Never use "I" in essays.

Proofread for Neatness
Q. Did you use the correct margins, double spacing, font, and paper?

Proofread for Outline
Q. Does your paper correspond to your original outline?

Proofread for Research
Q. Are your primary and secondary sources credible?

Proofread for Paper Format
Q. Does your paper have an Introduction, Body, and Conclusion?

Proofread for Thesis Statement
Q. Is your Thesis clearly stated in your introduction?

Proofread for Organization of Ideas
First give major points, and then give minor points.

Proofread for Redundancy
Q. Did you make the same point more than once?

Proofread for Writing Style
Q. Is your writing style appropriate for the required assignment, e.g., creative, scholarly or scientific?

Proofread for Facts
Q. Does your evidence really back up your argument? Is all the information relevant to your thesis statement?

Proofread for Paraphrasing
Q. Did you rewrite facts in your own words, and document sources?

Proofread for Fallacies (defects that weaken arguments):
Sweeping generalizations, appeal to authority, weak analogy, or ad populum.

Proofread for Quotes
Q. Are your quotes properly documented in an endnote, or in a footnote and in a bibliography?

Proofread for Citation Format
Q. Are your citations correctly formatted: APA, MLA, or Chicago

Let's Recap: **SMARTGRADES** Proofreading Checklist

Q. Did you set aside large blocks of time to proofread your paper to perfection?

Q. Did you enlarge the text to font size 18 to magnify your errors and make them easily visible?

Q. Did you choose font size 18 to find typos?

Q. Did you read your paper out loud to readily weed out all the errors?

Q. Did you purchase speech recognition software to cut in half the time it takes to proofread?

Q. Does paper correspond to your original outline?

Q. Does paper have an Introduction, Body, and Conclusion?

Q. Is your Thesis Statement clearly stated in your introduction?

Q. Is your writing style appropriate for the required assignment, e.g., creative, scholarly, or scientific?

Q. Does your evidence really back up your arguments?

Q. Is all the research relevant to your thesis statement?

Check Paraphrasing
Q. Did you rewrite the facts in your own words, and document the sources?

Check Fallacies (defects that weaken arguments)
(a) Sweeping generalizations
(b) Appeal to authority
(c) Weak analogy
(d) Ad populum

Check Quotes
Q. Are your quotes properly documented in an endnote or in a footnote and in a bibliography?

Check Paragraph Format
Q. Did you check for transition words, topic sentence, one main idea per paragraph, supporting example, quote from expert in the field, analysis and critical thinking skills, and concluding sentence?

Check Sentences
Q. Did you check for sentence fragments, run-ons, or comma splices (change punctuation or add conjunction).

Check Word Usage
Q. Did you use the thesaurus to find the best word to communicate your ideas and express your exact meaning?

Check Neatness
Q. Did you use the correct margins, double spacing, font, and paper?

**When You Take a Test,
You Are Really Being
Tested on Two Things:**

How Much You Know About the Subject

How Much You Know About Taking a Test

Chapter 9
Read, Memorize, and Test

"If any one faculty of our nature may be called more wonderful than the rest, I do think it is memory. There seems something more speakingly incomprehensible in the powers, the failures, the inequalities of memory, than in any other of our intelligences. The memory is sometimes so retentive, so serviceable, so obedient; at others, so bewildered and so weak; and at others again, so tyrannic, so beyond control! We are, to be sure, a miracle every way; but our powers of recollecting and of forgetting do seem peculiarly past finding out."

Jane Austen

Chapter 9
Read, Memorize, and Test

Tools of the Trade

Essay Exams

Multiple Choice Exams

True False Exams

Matching Exams

Fill in the Blank Exams

Oral Exams

Open Book Exams

Take Home Exams

Steps to Success

Step 1. The Day the Test is Announced

Q. Did you ask the teacher about the test?

a. What subjects are on the test?

b. What subjects are not on the test?

c. How many questions are on the test?

d. How is the test scored?

e. What kind of test is it?

Step 2. **Are You Prepared for the Right Type of Test?**
a. Essay Exam: Answer the question asked
b. Multiple Choice Exam: The answer is right in front of you
c. Oral Exam: Prepare for a personal interview format
d. Take Home Test: Apply **SMARTGRADES** Critical Thinking Tools for in-depth analysis of the academic material (Chapter 10).

Step 3. **Two Weeks Before the Test**
Q. Did you review your Test Review Notes? (Chapter 7).
Q. Did you self test to find your strengths and weaknesses?
Q. Did you visit the tutoring center to work out problems?
Q. Did you transform your weaknesses into strengths?
Q. Can you recall the facts for Instant Recall?
Q. Do you remember all of the facts for Total Recall?
Q. Did you change the association cues that do not work?

Step 4. **The Night Before the Test**
Q. Did you review Test Review Notes for Instant & Total Recall?
Q. Did you get 8 hours of deep sleep to feel energized?
Q. Did you prepare pens, pencils, sharpener, calculator, tissues, and clothing?
Q. Did you set your alarm clock?

Step 5. **Manage Your Test Anxiety**
Anxiety and stress are debilitating. They will ZAP your energy and destroy your ability to focus and concentrate on the test and you will draw blanks.

Q. Did you practice deep breathing exercises to be able to maintain a calm composure and relax?

The 3-Breath Method of Relaxation Breathing
- Get in a comfortable position, spine straight, feet flat on the floor. Close your eyes.
- Concentrate on your body, and notice where there is tension, discomfort or stress.
- Take a deep breath, visualize all your stress, then breathe out. While breathing out, visualize all the stress leaving your body.
- Repeat these steps at least three times.

Step 6. Develop Your Self-Esteem with Positive Self-Talk
Q. When you listen to your inner voice, do you hear positive supportive messages, e.g., "I have the strength to make my dreams come true." On a daily basis, you need to develop your self-esteem with positive self-talk.

Examples:
- Fear is only a feeling; it cannot hold me back

- I know that my potential is unlimited

- I have the strength to make my dreams come true

- I am proud of myself for even daring to try

- I grow in strength with every forward step I take

- I release my hesitation and make room for victory

Step 7. The Day of the Test

Q. Did you eat right (fiber fuel) for the energy to test?
   a. Breakfast of Champions: Oatmeal with Fresh Fruit
   b. Bran Muffin with Fresh Fruit

Q. Did you review your Test Review Notes to refresh your memory for Instant & Total Recall to ace your test?

The Day Before an Exam:
Prepare for the exam as if you are competing in an athletic event. Be well rested for the mental workout with a good night's sleep. Eat a high energy breakfast at least two hours before the exam, giving enough time for the body to digest the food. The day of the exam warm up the brain with a brief review. Arrive early. Relax. Compose your thoughts. Concentrate. Focus.

1. The Instructions:
First, listen carefully to oral instructions and then read all written instructions.

2. The Test Begins:
Jot down in the corner of the test everything you may forget during the test.

3. The Time:
Budget your time. Do not linger over difficult questions.

4. Your Mental, Emotional, and Spiritual Focus:
Concentrate on what you do know, don't worry about what you don't know.

5. The Question:
- Answer the questions you know first.
- Concentrate on one question at a time.
- Read each question completely before you begin to answer it.
- Answer question asked, not the one you may have expected.
- Go back to the ones you did not answer.
- Don't linger over difficult questions.
- Recall of the information you need may be triggered by completing other questions.

6. The Answer:
- Write down answer before reading choices.
- Read your answer choices carefully.
- Eliminate the choices that are clearly implausible.
- Don't search for hidden or extra meanings.
- Compare similarities & differences between choices.

Examine each word in answer for true or false possibility.
Key Words: All, Only, Always, Because = Generally False
Key Words: Few, Many, Much, Often, Many, Some, Perhaps, Generally = Possibly True
Break down complex sentences into smaller parts.
If small phrase = false, then entire statement = false.
If each word = false; then entire statement = false.

Change answers if you have a reason for doing so.
However do not change your answers based on a whim.
Use all the time allowed. If you finish early, proofread your paper for errors.

How to Ace Your Multiple Choice Test

Steps to Success

Step 1. Answer the easy questions first to build your confidence.

Step 2. Underline the key words in the question and try to answer the question. These tests rely on recognition, rather than recall.

Step 3. Think of multiple choice answers as a series of true or false statements. Read all of the choices even if the first choice seems correct. Compare similarities and differences between choices.

Step 4. Circle the absolute words in the question and the answer.

The absolutes are: all, none, always, never, only. These absolute words usually indicate a false choice.

Step 5. Circle the negative words in the question and the answer. Circle the negative words: not or except. These confusing questions cause careless errors. Mark each option with a T or F. Usually you are looking for a true statement. In this case, you are looking for a false statement.

Step 6. Find the dumb and dumber choices in the answer Cross out the two choices that are dumb and dumber. Examine the question and answer for clues.

Step 7. Change an answer when you have an intelligent reason to do so.

Beware the Dangers of Answer Sheets

Answer sheets allow exams to be scanned and marked automatically. Here are common mistakes to avoid:

1. Remember to record your name and student number on the actual answer sheet.

2. Use pencil so you can correct mistakes.

3. Do not cross out a mistake and mark another answer because the scanner will read this as "two" responses and record it as incorrect.

4. Always check your answers with the right question.

5. Consider marking your answers first on the exam paper, then transferring them to the answer sheet.

EVERY DAY AN EASY A

How to Ace Your Essay Test

Steps to Success

Step 1. Underline Key Word to Answer Question Asked

ANALYZE – Find the main ideas and show how they are related and why they are important.

COMMENT ON – Discuss, criticize, or explain its meaning as completely as possible.

COMPARE – Show both the similarities and differences.

CONTRAST – Show the differences.

CRITICIZE – Give your judgment or reasoned opinion of something, showing its good and bad points. It is not necessary to attack it.

DEFINE – Give the formal meaning by distinguishing it from related terms. This is often a matter of giving a memorized definition.

DESCRIBE – Write a detailed account or verbal picture in a logical sequence or story form.

DIAGRAM – Make a graph, chart, drawing. Be sure you label it and add a brief explanation if it is needed.

DISCUSS – Describe giving the details and explaining the pros and cons of it.

ENUMERATE — Name and list the main ideas one by one. Number them.

EVALUATE — Give your opinion or some expert's opinion of the truth or importance of the concept. Tell the advantages and disadvantages.

ILLUSTRATE — Explain or make it clear by concrete examples, comparison, or analogies.

INTERPRET — Give the meaning using examples and personal comments to make it clear.

JUSTIFY — Give a statement of why you think it is so. Give reasons for your statement or conclusion.

LIST — Produce a numbered list of words, sentences, or comments. Same as enumerate.

OUTLINE — Give a general summary. It should contain a series of main ideas supported by secondary ideas. Omit minor details. Show the organization of the ideas.

PROVE — Show by argument or logic that it is true. The word prove has a very special meaning in mathematics and physics.

RELATE — Show the connections between things, telling how one causes or is like another.

REVIEW — Give a survey or summary in which you look at the important parts and criticize where needed.

STATE — Describe the main points in precise terms. Be formal. Use brief, clear sentences. Omit details or examples.

SUMMARIZE — Give a brief, condensed account of the main ideas. Omit details and examples.

TRACE — Follow the progress or history of the subject.

Step 2. Restate Question as Introductory Sentence
Read the essay question and restate the question as the introductory sentence of your essay and add on the facts.

Example
Q. What are the most important issues your field is facing today?

A. The most important issues that my field is facing today are: Add main idea and major and minor ideas.

Step 3. Jot Down Main Ideas and Supporting Details
Jot down in the corner of the test the main ideas and supporting details to organize your thoughts before you write down the answer.

Main Ideas:
1.
2.
3.

Main Idea 1:
Supporting Details:
1. Expert in Field:
2. Indirect Quote:
3. Example:
4. Analysis:
5. Sum It Up:

Main Idea 2:
Supporting Details:
1. Expert in Field:
2. Indirect Quote:
3. Example:
4. Analysis:
5. Sum It Up:

Main Idea 3:
Supporting Details:
1. Expert in Field:
2. Indirect Quote:
3. Example:
4. Analysis:
5. Sum It Up:

Step 4. Use Standard Essay Structure
Use Introduction, Body, and Conclusion

Step 5. Use Standard Paragraph Structure

Sentence 1. Restate essay question ...

Sentence 2. According to Expert... (add quote)

Sentence 3. For example ... (proof)

Sentence 4. As a result ... (analysis)

Sentence 5. In conclusion ... (sum it up)

Step 6. Proofread Paper to Perfection
Proofread for spelling, punctuation, grammar, and neatness.

EVERY DAY AN EASY A

How to Ace Your True False Exam

Steps to Success

Step 1. Examine the Sentence

Every part of a true sentence must be "true." If any one part of the sentence is false, the whole sentence is false despite many other true statements. Long sentences often include groups of words set off by punctuation. Pay attention to the "truth" of each of these phrases. If one is false, it usually indicates a "false" answer.

Step 2. Underline Key Words

Pay close attention to negatives, qualifiers, absolutes, and long strings of statements.

Negatives: "No, Not, Cannot"
Qualifiers: "Sometimes, Often, Frequently, Ordinarily,
Absolutes: : "No, never, none, always, every, entirely, only"

Step 3. Guess True If You Are Unsure

Often true/false tests contain more true answers than false answers. You have more than 50% chance of being right with "true."

How to Ace Your Matching Exam

Steps to Success

Step 1. Use a Light Pencil

Mark them lightly with a pencil until you are completely done.

Step 2. Start with Matches that You Know Instantly

Step 3. Use a Darker Pencil

Make a second pass through matches, mark matches you are absolutely sure of with a darker penciled line.

Step 4. Search for Clues

Look for clues or relationships in the matches you aren't 100% sure of that you didn't think of the first time.

Step 5. Search for Other Possibilities

Look for another phrase that can be used instead of your first choice.

How to Ace Your Fill in the Blank Exam

Steps to Success

Step 1. This Exam Is the Most Difficult and Most Feared
You have to have the answers, such as names, places, and dates memorized for Instant & Total Recall.

Step 2. SMARTGRADES Processing Tools
Use the new learning technology, 10 Step **SMARTGRADES SUCCESS STRATEGY**, to process (absorb) the facts for Instant & Total Recall to ace every test every time.

Step 3. Answer the Easy Questions First

Step 4. Underline the Key Words in the Question

Step 5. Other Questions May Jog Your Memory
Sometimes, answers to questions you don't know are supplied in other questions.

Step 6. Educated Guess
The chances of getting a correct answer by writing down a wild guess is very slim, although not entirely unlikely.

How to Ace Your True False Exam

Steps to Success

Step 1. Examine the Sentence

Every part of a true sentence must be "true." If any one part of the sentence is false, the whole sentence is false, despite many other true statements. Long sentences often include groups of words set off by punctuation. Pay attention to the "truth" of each of these phrases. If one is false, it usually indicates a "false" answer.

Step 2. Underline Key Words

Pay close attention to negatives, qualifiers, absolutes, and long strings of statements.

Negatives: "No, Not, Cannot"
Qualifiers: "Sometimes, Often, Frequently, Ordinarily,
Absolutes: "No, never, none, always, every, entirely, only"

Step 3. Guess True If You Are Unsure

Often true/false tests contain more true answers than false answers. You have more than 50% chance of being right with "true."

How to Ace Your Open Book Exam

Steps to Success

Step 1. Use Textbook and Test Review Notes
Since you have already condensed the facts from your textbook into Test Review Notes, they are probably the fastest way to access the facts.

Step 2. Use Standard Essay Format
a. Write in complete sentences.
b. Restate the essay question as the introductory sentence and add on the facts.
c. Use an Introduction, Body, and Conclusion
d. Use transition words to bridge ideas:

Sentence 1. On one hand ... (the Pro argument)
　　　　　　　On the other hand ... (the Con argument)
Sentence 2. According to expert... (add quote)
Sentence 3. For example ...
Sentence 4. As a result ... (analysis)
Sentence 5. In conclusion ... (sum it up)

Step 3. Proofread to Perfection
Check for spelling, grammar, punctuation, and neatness.

How to Ace Your Take Home Exam

Steps to Success

Step 1. What Kinds of Material Can Be Used?
Take Home exams are unrestricted. The main restriction for Take Home exams is that they must be your work–you must attempt them by yourself without any help from others.

Step 2. What Do Take Home Exams Test?
They don't test your memory. They test your ability to find and use information for problem solving, and to deliver well-structured and well-presented arguments and solutions. They require you to apply knowledge rather than just remember facts.

Step 3. Follow the Instructions for Open Book Exams

Step 4. SMARTGRADES Critical Thinking Tools
To give a comprehensive analysis of the academic material, apply all of the **SMARTGRADES** Critical Thinking Tools (Chapter 10, p.195).

How to Ace Your Oral Exam

Steps to Success

Step 1. Create a Good Impression
- Dress well and appropriately
- Turn off your cell phone
- Arrive at the location early
- Review Test Review Notes to warm-up the facts

Step 2: Oral Exams Are Similar to Interviews
- Introduce yourself immediately and smile
- Give the instructor all of your attention
- Keep good posture and eye contact
- Stay focused through the exam
- Maintain your self-confidence and composure
- Be an intelligent listener as well as a talker
- Do not ramble if you do not know an answer
- If you do not know the answer, ask the teacher to ask the question in a different format to jog your memory
- Answer questions with more than "yes" or "no"
- Use two or three key points or examples to demonstrate your knowledge
- Thank the instructor

How to Transform an Exam Failure into a Success

You rushed through an exam, afraid that you will run out of time, and made careless mistakes:

- You misread the questions
- You misread the directions
- You blackened the wrong box on an answer sheet
- You skipped a question or two
- You forgot to write legibly

Steps to Success

Step 1. Ask for a REDO!
An instructor may allow you to rewrite an essay exam, rework a math problem from the original question, and improve your grade. The worst they are going to say is no.

Step 2. Ask for Extra Credit Work
Ask for extra credit work to make up for a poor performance on a key exam.

Step 3. Review Mistakes
All knowledge bases are cumulative. Sometimes you get a problem wrong because you didn't understand the subject as well as you thought. After an exam fill in your knowledge gaps, to be prepared for the next test.

Step 4. Talk to Your Teacher
Ask your instructor for an explanation of your grade or comment. Use this as a time to find out how you can do better next time. Keep track of your strengths and weaknesses.

What Is the Hardest Task in the World?
To Think.

Ralph Waldo Emerson

Chapter 10
Critical Thinking Skills

The Trouble with the World
Is that the Stupid Are Cocksure and
the Intelligent Are Full of Doubt.

Bertrand Russell

THERE IS ONLY ONE
TRUTH
NO ONE HAS THE TRUTH

Sharon Esther Lampert

Chapter 10
Critical Thinking Skills

Tools of the Trade

1. Read with an Open Mind
2. Read with a Critical Mind
3. Evaluate the Underlying Assumptions
4. Read for Arguments Based on Fallacies
5. Read for Inductive and Deductive Reasoning

Steps to Success

Step 1. Read with an Open Mind
Develop mental flexibility, a willingness to think clearly and weigh all sides of every question. To resolve a problem, attack a problem with an open mind. Prepare to consider all possibilities and probe the issue to the heart.

Step 2. Read with a Critical Mind
Separate the facts of the story (verifiable evidence) from the opinions of the author. Caution: Some facts, such as statistical surveys and historical events are based on "opinions."

Step 3. Evaluate the Underlying Assumptions
Assumptions are the set of belief systems that are considered to be self-evident.

Step 4. Read for Arguments Based on Fallacies
Learn to recognize the presentation of misleading evidence that is false.

Misdirected Appeals: Appeal to authority, appeal to common or popular belief, appeal to common practice or tradition, appeal to indirect consequences, appeal to wishful thinking.

Emotional Appeals: Appeal to fear or scare tactics, appeal to force, appeal to loyalty or peer pressure, appeal to pity or sob story, appeal to prejudice, appeal to stereotypes, appeal to hatred, appeal to vanity.

Step 5. Read for Inductive and Deductive Reasoning
Induction argues from observation from the specific to the general. Deduction argues from the general to the specific (rules and laws).

A Checklist for Critical Thinking Tools

Q. Did you read with an open mind?

Q. Did you think clearly and weigh all sides of every question?

Q. Did you resolve a problem, and attack a problem with a flexible mind?

Q. Did you consider all possibilities and probe the issue to the heart?

Q. Did you read with a critical mind and separate the facts of the story (verifiable evidence) from the opinions of the author.

Q. Did you evaluate the underlying assumptions?

Q. Did you read for arguments based on fallacies?

Misdirected Appeals:
1. Appeal to authority
2. Appeal to common or popular belief
3. Appeal to common practice or tradition
4. Appeal to indirect consequences
5. Appeal to wishful thinking

Emotional Appeals:
1. Appeal to fear or scare tactics
2. Appeal to force
3. Appeal to loyalty or peer pressure
4. Appeal to pity or sob story
5. Appeal to prejudice
6. Appeal to stereotypes
7. Appeal to hatred
8. Appeal to vanity

Q. Did you read for inductive and deductive reasoning?

> If I Create from the Heart,
> Nearly Everything Works;
> If from the Head Almost Nothing!
> Marc Chagall

Critical Thinking	Creative Thinking
analytic	generative
convergent	divergent
vertical	lateral
probability	possibility
judgment	suspended judgment
focused	diffuse
objective	subjective
answer	answers
left brain	right brain
verbal	visual
linear	associative
reasoning	richness, novelty
yes but	yes and

Chapter 11
WORLD PREMIERE!
Creative Thinking Tools

SEE THE WORLD THROUGH THE EYES OF A CREATIVE GENIUS

POE**T**REE

Ink needs a pen.
Pen needs paper.
Paper needs a poem.
Poem needs a poet.
Poet needs a muse.
Muse needs a poet.
Poet needs divine inspiration.
Divine inspiration needs divine intervention.
Divine intervention needs divine grace.
Divine grace needs immortality.
Immortality needs eternity.
Eternity needs readers of poetry.

Sharon Esther Lampert
V.E.S.S.E.L.: VERY. EXTRA. SPECIAL. SHARON. ESTHER. LAMPERT.

"Please Handle My Poems Gently.
These Poems Are My Remains."
Sharon Esther Lampert

www.WorldFamousPoems.com
The Greatest Poems Ever Written on Extraordinary World Events

Chapter 11
WORLD PREMIERE!
Creative Thinking Tools

10 Tools of the Trade

1. V.E.S.S.E.L.
2. INSPIRATION
3. IMPREGNATION
4. INCUBATION
5. GENESIS
6. SILENT:LISTEN
7. METAMORPHOSIS
8. REVELATION
9. SIGNATURE
10. IMMORTALITY

Read: "Unleash The Creator, The God Within: 10 Esoteric Laws of Genius & Creativity"

Steps to Success

Step 1. V.E.S.S.E.L.
Keep an open mind and heart, so that you can receive inspirations that come from everywhere. Artistic gifts are inherited. There are good, great, and gifted **ARTISTS.**

Step 2. INSPIRATION
When something moves you emotionally, and transforms your inner world in such a way that you feel differently, think differently, and see differently — that external force is called inspiration. Inspiration is everywhere!

Step 3. IMPREGATION (ARTIST & ARTWORK BECOME ONE)
You are inspired and become impregnated with an idea.

Step 4. INCUBATION
The **ARTWORK** resides within the **ARTIST** and grows quietly over time. There is no such thing as "Writer's Block." It is a myth. You must be patient and allow **ARTWORK** to incubate within you.

Step 5. GENESIS (ARTIST & ARTWORK BECOME TWO)
When **ARTWORK** is ready to be born, it takes on a life of its own, separates from the **ARTIST**, and has its own destiny (mission, message, and meaning) e.g., music composition.

Step 6. SILENT: LISTEN
The **ARTIST** remains silent and listens within to the **ARTWORK**.

Step 7. METAMORPHOSIS: MISSION, MEANING, MESSAGE
The **ART** and the **ARTIST** are now two separate entities. The **ART** and the **ARTIST** have to be nurtured for both of them to grow and reach maturity.

Step 8. REVELATION: MESSAGE
The **ART** touches other people with its own message, and has its distinct own destiny, separate from the **ARTIST**.

Step 9. SIGNATURE
The **ART** bears the autograph of the **ARTIST**.

Step 10. IMMORTALITY
ARTWORK lives beyond the life of the **ARTIST**.
ARTIST IS MORTAL. ART IS IMMORTAL.

Steps to Success

Most creative people credit their vivid imaginations for their success, e.g., J.K. Rowling and Harry Potter.

Q. Do you have the emotional, spiritual, and intellectual fortitude to express your ideas without fear from shame and ridicule?

Q. Do you have a vivid imagination?

Q. Do you write down your wild'n'crazy ideas and let them mature into a poem, a play, or a novel?

Q. Are you a daydreamer? Do you write down your daydreams?

Q. Do you let your mind flow freely to associate and brainstorm for ideas?

DAILY ACTION PLAN
Creative thinking requires thinking "outside the box." Start a creative ideas journal. List all ideas that come to mind, no matter how bizarre, weird, or strange, and see where they take you. Perhaps a novel will emerge, or a poem, or a plot for a movie script or even a play.

Research Is What I'm Doing
When I Don't Know What I'm Doing

Wernher Von Braun

Chapter 12
Scientific Thinking Tools

Chapter 12
Scientific Thinking Tools

The scientific method is a process for experimentation that is used to explore observations that use the five senses, and to answer questions about the natural world. Scientists use the scientific method to search for cause and effect relationships in nature. An experiment is designed so that changes to one item cause something else to vary in a predictable way. The sciences rely heavily on numbers as data, and on replicable experimentation to measure and calculate results.

Tools of the Trade

The Scientific Method
- Make Observations By Using Your 5 Senses
- Ask Questions
- Perform Experiments
- Collect Data
- Measure Data
- Classify Data
- Make a Hypothesis
- Interpret Data
- Analyze Information
- Draw Conclusions
- Make a Prediction
- Verification of Experiment

The Science Report

Section 1   Title Page
Section 2   Abstract
Section 3   Table of Contents
Section 4   Question, Variables, and Hypothesis
Section 5   Background Research
Section 6   Materials List
Section 7   Experimental Procedure
Section 8   Data Analysis and Discussion
Section 9   Conclusions
Section 10   Ideas for Future Research
Section 11   Acknowledgements
Section 12   Bibliography

Q. What Is Scientific Thinking?
Scientific (and critical) thinking is based on three things:

1. **Empiricism:** Using empirical evidence found in nature. Using evidence that is found in nature. It is evidence that is perceptible from the senses; evidence that one can see, hear, touch, taste, or smell.

2. **Rationalism:** Practicing logical reasoning

3. **Skepticism:** Possessing a skeptical attitude about presumed knowledge that leads to self-questioning, holding tentative conclusions, and being undogmatic (willingness to change one's beliefs).

WORLD PEACE EQUATION

VG+VL=VP

Virtue of the Good + Value of Life = Vision of Peace

The Mathematical and Philosophical Proof for World Peace

$$VG + VL = VP$$
$$VP = VG + VL$$
$$VP = V(G+L)$$
$$P = (G+L)$$
$$Peace = Good + Life$$
$$Peace = Goodlife$$

PHOTON
SUPERHERO OF EDUCATION
www.BooksNotBombs.com

SMART POWER IS BACK IN THE HANDS OF ALL STUDENTS

Chapter 13
Mathematical Thinking Skills

The Highest Form of Pure Thought Is in Mathematics

Plato
Ancient Greek Philosopher
428 BC-348 BC

Chapter 13
Mathematical Thinking Skills

Math is learned by solving many types of problems. Math is cumulative. Every class builds on the previous one.

Tools of the Trade

Solving Math Problems
1. Think in steps: Step by step
2. Memorize the fundamentals
3. Translate abstract concepts into concrete terms

Ask Questions
1. What is given?
2. What is called for?
3. How many steps are required?
4. What operation must be used in each step?
5. Are the steps in the right order?
6. Check answer and make sure it is right

Math Errors
20% of All Math Errors Are Careless Mistakes
1. Write each number legibly
2. Place two columns of figures exactly under one another
3. Copy each problem correctly

Steps to Success

In-Class Math Strategy: Take Organized Math Notes
Keep a list of the types of math problems solved and the sequence of steps:

Math Problem Type   Equations Used   Sequence of Steps

- As questions arise, ask your teacher for clarification.
- Don't leave class feeling lost, confused, and hopeless.

At-Home Math Strategy: Rework Class Problems
After every class, review your class notes and rework the math problems covered in class

Step 1. Write Out the Math Problem
- Read the word problem slowly and carefully.

- Remember this adage: Go slow to go fast.

- Slow is the way to accuracy and great grades.

- Write out the problem, number the steps, and double check what you've written.

- What are you trying to figure out? The last sentence of a word problem tells you what you are trying to find.

Step 2. Write Down the Information in the Problem

| Data | Variable | Equation |

Word problems contain all the information needed to answer the question.

- List all the information given in the problem.

- Make two lists: Separate the knowns from the unknowns (the variable).

| **Knowns** | **Unknowns** |

Q. What is the relationship between the known and the unknown values?

- Write an equation.

- Solve for the unknowns.

Step 3. What is the Best Math Method?

Make a plan and solve the problem. Develop a plan to solve the problem and solve it according to your plan.

Q1. How many steps does it take to solve the problem?

Q2. Does one part of the problem have to be solved before other parts can be solved?

Q3. Can the problem be divided into parts and solved separately?

Step 4. Check Your Work and Reread the Problem

- Check to see that you did not leave out any steps of your plan.
- Read problem again to see if your answer makes sense.
- Check answers for careless mistakes.
- Double check your calculator work immediately.

Step 5. Math Test Success Strategy

- Solve unassigned homework problems and see if you can finish them in the allotted time for the exam.
- Write big and bold. This will allow you to see a mistake and keep from confusing numbers, letters, or signs. Careless errors often creep in because you don't give yourself enough space to see and solve the problem.
- Answer the easy questions first to build your confidence. Budget your time.
- If you get stuck on a problem move on and come back to it later.
- Don't leave if you finish the exam early. Go back to the difficult problems.
- Use all of the available time to look for careless errors.

If You Think Dogs Can't Count,
Try Putting Three Dog Biscuits in Your
Pocket, and Then Giving Fido
Only Two of Them.

Phil Pastoret

Little Johnny

Little Johnny was sitting in class doing math problems when his teacher picked him to answer a question, "Johnny, if there were five birds sitting on a fence and you shot one with your gun, how many would be left?" "None," replied Johnny, "cause the rest would fly away." "Well, the answer is four," said the teacher, "but I like the way you're thinking."

Be Nice to Nerds!
Chances Are, You'll End Up Working for One!

Bill Gates
CEO of Microsoft

Chapter 14

What Do You Want to Be When You Grow Up

Follow Your Passion,
Fulfill Your Potential, and
Find Your Place in the World

PHOTON
SUPERHERO OF EDUCATION
EVERYBODY IS SOMEBODY SPECIAL
www.PhotonSuperhero.com

Chapter 14

What Do You Want to Be When You Grow Up

Everybody is somebody special. Before you can find out how special you are, you have to figure out your strengths and weaknesses.

My Strengths Are:
1. _____
2. _____
3. _____

My Weaknesses Are:
1. _____
2. _____
3. _____

Once you have a clear picture of yourself, you will then be able to make choices that lead you in the direction of your dreams. For example, if you love science because you want to know how the natural world works, then you will probably read a lot of books about biology, chemistry, and physics. The key to success is to align your personality with a career that will become your life's work and passion. Everyone in the world does the same thing, that is, everyone is a "caretaker" of something in the world. Some people become florists because they like to care for flowers. Some people become mechanics because they love to care for cars. To find your passion, ask yourself this simple question: Q: What do want to take care of?

My Passion Is: _____.

EVERY DAY AN EASY A

How to Choose a Career That Fits Your Personality Type

Read through the lists below for careers that are interesting to you and that will need futher exploration to acertain whether you are well suited based on your intellectual and emotional strengths and weaknesses.

Hands-On Career Choices (for the physically active)
Air Traffic Controller, Archaeologist, Athletic Trainer, Carpenter, Caterer, Cartographer, Chef, Computer Repairs Engineer Construction Worker, Dental Technician, Drafter, Electrician, Farm Manager, Firefighter, Fish and Game Warden, Forester, Hairdresser, Landscape Architect, Licensed Practical Nurse, Locksmith, Mechanic, Machinist, Military Officer, Physical Therapist, Police Officer, Plumber, Recreation Administrator, Surveyor, Teacher, Truck Driver, X-Ray Technician

Helper Career Choices
(working with people, good communicators)
Airline Personnel, Athletic Coach, Attorney, Career Counselor, Chamber of Commerce Claims Adjuster, Child Care Worker, Cosmetologist, Counselor, Dietitian, Fitness Instructor, Funeral Director, Home Health Aide, Information Clerk, Occupational Therapist, Mental Health Specialist, Nurse, Office Worker Paramedic, Parole Officer, Personnel Director, Physical Therapist, Receptionist, Recreation Director, Religious Worker, Teacher, Therapist, Travel Agent, Sales Representative, Social Worker, Waiter/Waitress, Youth Service Worker

Investigator Career Choices
(curious, logical, think independently, work alone)
Astronomer, Biologist, College Professor, Computer Analyst, Computer System Analyst, Consumer Researcher, Dentist, Dietitian, Ecologist, Engineer, Horticulturist, Lawyer, Librarian, Medical Technologist, Meteorologist, Nurse, Paralegal, Pharmacist, Physician, Police Detective, Reporter, Research Analyst, Science Lab Technician, Science/Math Teacher, Technical Writer, Veterinarian

Helper Career Choices
(working with people, good communicators)
Airline Personnel, Athletic Coach, Attorney Career Counselor, Chamber of Commerce Claims Adjuster, Child Care Worker, Cosmetologist, Counselor, Dietitian, Fitness Instructor, Funeral Director, Home Health Aide Information Clerk, Occupational Therapist Mental Health Specialist, Nurse, Office Worker Paramedic, Parole Officer, Personnel Director Physical Therapist, Receptionist, Recreation Director, Religious Worker, Teacher, Therapist, Travel Agent, Sales Representative, Social Worker, Waiter/Waitress, Youth Service Worker

Enterprise Career Choices
(outgoing, self-confident, sociable, adventurous)
Advertising Agent, Advertising Executive, Announcer, Banker, Business Manager, Campaign Manager, Entrepreneur, Florist, Insurance Manager, Lawyer, Lobbyist, Office Manager, Personnel Recruiter, Police Officer, Politician, Real Estate Appraiser, Sales Person, Stock Broker, Travel Agent, TV/Radio

Artist Career Choices
(self-expression, imaginative, innovative)

Advertising Manager, Architect, Artist, Cartographer, Cosmetologist, Dance Instructor, Drama Coach, English Teacher, Entertainer, Florist, Graphic Designer, Interior Decorator, Illustrator, Journalist, Landscaper, Librarian, Lighting Specialist, Museum Curator, Music Teacher, Musician, Painter, Photographer Recording Technician, Reporter, Writer

Science Career Choices
(curious, logical, think independently, work alone)

Aerospace Engineer, Astronomer, Aviation Inspector, Athletic Trainer, Biochemist, CAD Technician, Chemist, Civil Engineer, Computer Hardware Engineer, Computer Programmer, Computer Software Engineer, Diver, Electrical Engineer Electrician, Environmental Engineer, Food Science Technician Food Scientist or Technologist, Genetic Counselor, Geographer, Geologist, Industrial Engineer, Marine Architect, Mechanical Engineer, Medical and Clinical Laboratory Technician, Meteorologist, Microbiologist, Multi-Media Artist or Animator, Natural Sciences Manager, Physicist, Pilot, Plant Scientist, Psychologist, Ship and Boat Captain, Sociologist, Sound Engineering Technician, Statistician, Veterinarian, Zoologist, Wildlife Biologist.

Detailers Career Choices
(steady routines, defined procedures, collecting and organizing)

Accountant, Actuary, Administrative Assistant, Auditor Statistician, Bank Manager, Business Teacher, Librarian, Bookkeeper, Cartographer, Cashier, Credit Manager, CAD Operator, Coat Analyst, Corrections Officer, Computer Operator, Court Reporter, Estimator, Financial Analyst, Hotel Clerk, Insurance Underwriter, Medical Lab Technologist, Medical Secretary, Personnel Clerk, Secretary, Paralegal, Proofreader, Reservations Agent, Safety Inspector, Tax Consultant

Know Thyself
1. What type of career is best suited to your personality type?

2. What social causes are you most concerned about?

3. If you could change something in the world, what would it be?

4. Where do you think you can make a difference?

5. When kinds of books do you love to read?

What If you could solve just one problem in this world and by solving that one problem you could solve every problem in the world?

If we just solve the "problem of education," then we could solve every problem in the world: poverty, illiteracy, domestic violence, religious strife, and war.

The human brain is the most powerful biological machine in the world. What would the world look like if educators knew how to nurture and cultivate the awesome power of the human brain?

When the seeds of peace are planted within the minds and hearts of our children, through education, then and only then, will there be peace on earth. Our children are our only hope for peace in the world, and education is the only path to peace.

Sharon Rose Sugar
The Paladin of Education for the 21st Century

THIS BOOK SAVES LIVES
"The Silent Crisis Destroying America's Brightest Minds"
"Book of the Month" Alma Public Library, Wisconsin

About Us

SMARTGRADES
BRAIN POWER REVOLUTION

Sharon Rose Sugar
The Paladin of Education for the 21st Century

Critical Contributions to Education

1. **SMARTGRADES BRAIN POWER REVOLUTION**
2. Education Paradigm: The Learning-Processing Education System
3. 40 Universal Gold Standards of Education
4. How to Nurture and Cultivate the Power of the Human Brain
5. How Does Learning Take Place
6. How to Measure Education

7. 8 Goalposts of Education:
   1. EDUCATION: KNOWLEDGE!
   2. ENLIGHTENMENT: AHA!
   3. EMPOWERMENT: YES I CAN!
   4. EXCELLENCE: MASTERY!
   5. EMANCIPATION: ALL CAN DO!
   6. EGALITARIANISM: EQUAL RIGHTS!
   7. EQUALITY: NEW WORLD ORDER!
   8. ECONOMIC STABILITY: WORLD PEACE!

8. Integration Therapy for Intrapersonal Growth, Development, and Maturity: 13 Steps to True and Everlasting Happiness

9. Feed the Whole Child: Mind, Body, and Spirit
10. Spiritual Affirmations: Empowerment, Responsibility, Special Gifts

11. The Silent Crisis Destroying America's Brightest Minds
    - 15 Stumbling Blocks of Academic Failure
    - 15 Stepping Stones to Academic Success
    - Downward Spiral of Academic Failure
    - Academic Insanity
    - Misdiagnosis of A.D.H.D., "The Incurable Brain Disorder"

12. The 3 Stages of Child Abuse: Cripple, Parasite, and Predator

13. Coined Word, "Democrisy," a Democracy Laden with Hypocrisy

14. **PHOTON SUPERHERO OF EDUCATION,** PhotonSuperhero.com

15. C.A.P.S. Children's Science Curriculum, Grades 1-4 (Content, Activity, Process, and Society)

16. In One Hour, Read Hebrew, HebrewPowerHour.com

Thinkers in Education

One Small Step for Women and One Giant Leap Forward for Education and World Peace.

Alain, Aristotle, Avicenna, Bello, Bettelheim, Binet, Blonsky, Al-Boustani, Buber, Cai Yuanpei, Claparede, Comenious, Condorcet, Confucius, Cousinet, Dawid, Decroly, Dewey, Diesterweg, Durkheim, Eotvos, Erasmus, Al-Farabi, Ferriere, Freinet, Freire, Freud, Frobel, Fukuzawa, Gandhi, Al-Ghazali, Giner de los Rios, Glinos, Goodman, Gramsci, Grundtvig, Grzegorzewska, Hegel, Herbart, Humbolt, Husen, Hussein, Illich, Jaspers, Jovellanos, Jullien de Paris, Kandel, Kant, Kerschensteiner, Key, Ibn Khaldun, Kold, Korczak, Krupskaya, Locke, Makarenko, Marti, Mencious, Miskawayh, Montaigne, Montessori, More, Naik, Neill, Noikov, Nyerere, Ortega y Gasset, Owen, Pestalozzi, Piaget, Plato, Priestley, Al-Qabbani, Read, Rogers, Rousseau, Rudenschold, Sadler, Salomon, Sarmiento, Sergio, Skinner, Spencer, Steiner, Suchodolski,
**Sharon Rose Sugar (Sharon Esther Lampert)
PHOTON SUPERHERO OF EDUCATION,**
Sun Yat-Sen, Tagore, Al-Tahtawi, Tolstoy, Trefort, Trstenjak, Ushinsky, Uznadze, Varela, Vasconcelos, Vico, Vives, Vygotsky, Wallon

The Official Emblem of

PHOTON

Super Hero Refresher Course

Clark Kent Is Superman

Bruce Wayne Is Batman

Peter Parker Is Spiderman

Diana Themyscira Is Wonder Woman

Sharon Rose Sugar Is Photon

SEE THE WORLD THROUGH THE EYES OF A CREATIVE GENIUS

POETRY WORLD RECORD
120 WORDS OF RHYME FROM ONE FAMILY OF RHYME
Bible: "Through the Eyes of Eve"

THE WORLD TRADE CENTER TRAGEDY
"Spiraling Downward, Upward We Stand United"

Dr. Martin Luther King Jr.
"THE DELIVERER"

SIMON WIESENTHAL: NAZI HUNTER
"A Survivor's Burden"

Bible: CAIN & ABEL
"Cain & Abel: Inseparable-Together Forever"

"TSUNAMI" (Poet's Personal Favorite)

SUICIDE BOMBERS
"The Militant Palestinian Toddler Terrorist"

DARFUR
"There Is No Flower in Darfur"

THE IRAQ WAR
"Sandstorm in Baghdad"

KANSAS TWISTER
"The Return of Dorothy Gale"

KATRINA
"Drowning in the American Dream"

CENTRAL PARK VIOLENCE AGAINST WOMEN
"Water, Fight, Flight, and Tears"
(most published poem on the internet)

THE NEW YORK CITY BLACKOUT
"The Return of the Cavewoman"

Does Your Kid Read Sharon Esther Lampert?

Critical Contributions to Civilization

The Prodigy
Unleash The Creator The God Within
10 Esoteric Laws of Genius & Creativity

The Awesome Art of Alliteration
Using One Letter of the Alphabet

The Prophet
Who Knew God Was Such a Chatterbox

THE 22 COMMANDMENTS
All You Will Ever Need to Know About God

The Philosopher Queen
- God of What? 11 Esoteric Laws of Inextricability
- The Sperm Manifesto: 10 Rules for the Road
- Women Have All The Power —
  But Have Never Learned How to Use It

The Poet
- I Stole All The Words from The Dictionary

- **IMMORTALITY IS MINE**
  The Greatest Poems Ever Written on Extraordinary World Events

- **POETRY JEWELS**
  Diamonds, Emeralds, Sapphires, Rubies, and Pearls

- **V.E.S.S.E.L.**
  Very. Extra. Special. Sharon. Esther. Lampert.

How to Read a Poem By Sharon Esther Lampert

1. Similar to the poet William Blake, Sharon's poems are accompanied by elaborate visual graphics that enrich and compliment the text.

2. Sharon is a master of the art of condensation. She is able to condense a major world event in world history into a one page poem.

3. Sharon's poems are telescopic of the main event and microscopic of the infinite details.

4. Sharon's poems are known for her ability to weave poetry, philosophy, and comedy into a single verse.

5. Sharon's poems take you on a cinematic journey, and make you feel as if you are reliving the event, as if it happened today.

6. Many poets leave abandoned poems, that are unfinished. Sharon's poems are completed works of art. Every word is essential to the poem. You cannot remove or replace a word. There are no extra words. Every word has its rightful place and fits to perfection.

7. Sharon's poems are inspired. There are no rough drafts. Like giving birth to a baby, the poem incubates in her "creative apparatus" and is birthed in minutes. Like a baby, the poems are delivered whole and complete.

8. The last verse of every poem delivers a message that educates, enlightens, and empowers. Her searing signature endings seep under your skin, and find a way into your heart, and open your mind to a deeper understanding of the world.

Letter from Mommy, Age 9
Darling Sharon,
My Daughter is a Poet, Philosopher, and Teacher.
Beauty & Brains.
Love and Kisses, XXX
Mommy (Eve Lampert)

SHARON ESTHER LAMPERT

The Sole Intention of My Poetry Is to Add Light to Your Soul.
Sharon Esther Lampert

SEE THE WORLD THROUGH THE EYES OF A CREATIVE GENIUS

APRIL 30
N.Y.C. Poetry In Your Pocket Day

BE BORN

Be Born.
Become Educated.
Love Your Work.
Make a Meaningful Contribution -
to Yourself, Your Family, and Humanity.
Be a True Friend to Yourself First.
Have Sex with Someone You Love.
Make Love with Complete Abandon.
Enjoy Unconditional Love from Your Devoted Pet.
Make Time to Read the Funnies and Laugh.
Save Enough Money to Visit the Popular,
Pretty, and Peaceful Places of the World.
Read Great Literature, Listen to Great Music,
See Great Art, Watch the Great Movies,
Play the Fun Sports, Dance till Dawn,
Taste the Great Culinary Delights of the World -
Eat Slowly, Enjoy Every Bite, and Stay in Shape.
Plan One Great Adventure and Stick to the Plan.
Grow Old and Wise. Leave Your Money to
Someone You Love - Who Loves You Back.
Die in Your Sleep.

Sharon Esther Lampert

www.WorldFamousPoems.com
The Greatest Poems Ever Written on Extraordinary World Events

The Sole Intention of My Poetry Is to Add LIGHT to Your Soul

SEE THE WORLD THROUGH THE EYES OF A CREATIVE GENIUS

THE 22 COMMANDMENTS
ALL YOU WILL EVER NEED TO KNOW ABOUT GOD
A UNIVERSAL MORAL COMPASS FOR ALL PEOPLE,
FOR ALL RELIGIONS, AND FOR ALL TIME

1. LIFE Over Death
2. STRENGTH Over Weakness
3. DEED Over Sin
4. LOVE Over Hatred
5. TRUTH Over Lie
6. WISDOM Over Stupidity
7. OPTIMISM Over Pessimism
8. SHARING Over Selfishness
9. PRAISE Over Criticism
10. LOYALTY Over Abandonment
11. RESPONSIBILITY Over Blame
12. GRATITUDE Over Envy
13. REWARD Over Punishment
14. ALLIES Over Enemies
15. CREATION Over Destruction
16. EDUCATION Over Ignorance
17. COOPERATION Over Competition
18. FREEDOM Over Oppression
19. COMPASSION Over Indifference
20. FORGIVENESS Over Revenge
21. PEACE Over War
22. JOY Over Suffering

Sharon Esther Lampert
Kadimah: 8th Prophetess of Israel

www.PoetryJewels.com
Diamonds, Emeralds, Sapphires, Rubies, and Pearls

The Sole Intention of My Poetry Is to Add LIGHT to Your Soul

PHOTON
SUPERHERO of EDUCATION®

EVERY DAY AN EASY A

EVERY DAY AN EASY A
3 Editions: Elementary, High School, College
ACE EVERY TEST EVERY TIME
All Global Bookstores

www.BooksNotBombs.com
EVERYBODY IS SOMEBODY SPECIAL

1 Minute Time Management Class
10 Steps to Success

PHOTON INC. All Rights Reserved. 2010

Step 1 ☐
Make a Daily Action Plan
Write Down Your Big Goals

Step 2 ☐
Set Your Priorities
Urgent, Important, Low, and Optional

Step 3 ☐
Breakdown Your Dreams
Breakdown Big Goal into Smaller Steps
List Steps Necessary to Complete Big Goal

Step 4 ☐
Divide and Conquer
Take Baby Steps Toward Reaching Goal
Crawl. Walk. Fly. Soar...

Step 5 ☐
Use Time Logs: Estimated Vs. Actual Time
e.g., Estimate Time for Lunch: 1 Hour
Actual Time: 20 Minutes
40 Minutes for Errands: Bank, Post Office, Store

Step 6 ☐
Life Is a Bumpy Road
Make Time for Delays, Detours,
Distractions, and Disappointments
e.g., Copier Runs Out of Toner and Paper

Step 7 ☐
Use Checkboxes to Keep Track of Completed Tasks

Step 8 ☐
Review and Refine Daily Action Plan
Pay Attention to Strengths and Weaknesses

Step 9 ☐
Celebrate Your Success
Celebrate Job Well Done with Daily Reward

Step 10 ☐
EVERY DAY AN EASY A
www.everydayaneasya.com

www.ingramcontent.com/pod-product-compliance
Lightning Source LLC
Chambersburg PA
CBHW042135160426
43200CB00019B/2942